STREET MAGIC

THIS IS A CARLTON BOOK

DEDICATION
This book is dedicated to Madame Pat Thompson of Bermagui, Australia, a truly
inspirational lady – when I think of the word "spirit", I think of you. Love ya girl!
PZ xxx

Text copyright © Paul Zenon 2005
Design and photographs © Carlton Books Limited 2005

A CIP catalogue record for this book is available from the British Library

ISBN 978-1-84732-562-4

Printed in Singapore

Project Editor: Roland Hall
Art Direction: Darren Jordan
Designer: Simon Osborne
Production: Lisa French & Claire Hayward

Photography: Karl Adamson (tricks), Rich Hardcastle (all chapter openers and 5, 47, 133)

ACKNOWLEDGEMENTS
The publishers would like to thank The Mortimer, Mortimer Street, London W1 and The Prince Albert, Trafalgar
Street, Brighton BN1 for their kind assistance.

PICTURE CREDITS
P6: www.bridgeman.co.uk
P7: L: Mary Evans Picture Library, R: Mary Evans/Harry Price
P8: L: Mary Evans Picture Library, R: Charles Walker/Topfoto
P11: T: Getty Images/Scott Gries/ImageDirect, B: Paul Zenon.
Every effort has been made to acknowledge correctly and contact the source and/or copyright holder of each
picture and Carlton Books Ltd apologizes for any unintentional errors or omissions which will be corrected in
future editions of this book.

PAUL ZENON

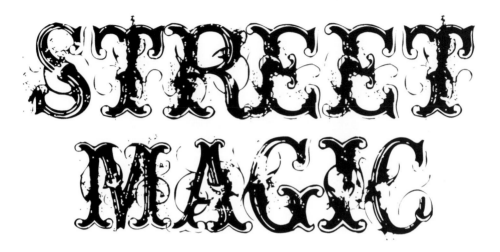

STREET MAGIC

GREAT TRICKS AND CLOSE-UP
SECRETS REVEALED

CARLTON

CONTENTS

INTRODUCTION

What is Street Magic?

If you'd asked that question only a few years ago, the answer would have been very simple. A street magician was a busker; someone who would work in town squares, marketplaces and festivals drawing a crowd, giving a performance and then passing round a hat to collect money for their efforts. However, this is not a book about busking. Nowadays, in the eyes of the public, the term "street magic" is more likely to relate to the world of hit-and-run close-up illusion they see on slickly-produced television specials. On those television shows the performer specializes in a kind of guerilla magic, going up to complete strangers and proceeding to freak them out with a series of mind-blowing tricks – money appears from nowhere, playing cards defy the laws of physics, minds are read, the impossible happens right under your nose. The magic happens without the help of special equipment, trapdoors, mirrors

The Conjuror by Hieronymus Bosch, c.1500. My great, great, great, great grandad is the one stealing the guy's purse on the left.

Mr Lane, a conjuror at London's Bartholomew Fair, 17th Century.

A French street magician peforming the famous Cups and Balls trick, c.1805.

or glamorous assistants. It happens with ordinary objects in everyday surroundings – in cafes and bars, at bus stops and on street corners. These television specials have helped establish magic not just as one of the most popular forms of entertainment in the world, but also one of the coolest.

Magic has always had international apppeal, crossing cultural boundaries as easily as Houdini walked through walls, but the advent of television has meant that a small trick that would be lost on a big theatre stage can fill the screen in millions of households worldwide. The pioneers of this new style of televised magic such as David Blaine, Criss Angel, Derren Brown and, I hope, myself, brought magic to new audiences, audiences that wouldn't usually be found in a theatre, cabaret club, cruise ship lounge or television studio. The use of a single hand-held camera seemed to make the use of camera trickery impossible and gave the magic an edgy and immediate feel – the viewer feels that they are experiencing the magic exactly as if they were there in the street with the other amazed onlookers.

The Magician's Craft

Although the style of presentation has changed, many of the tricks used by today's most famous television magicians have their roots in the acts of those street magicians of old. Tricks are like fine wines; they improve with age as every generation adds a new touch to make them stronger and more baffling.

One of the earliest descriptions of the work of street magicians is contained in Reginald Scot's *Discoverie of Witchcraft*, published in 1584. Scot was a magistrate and he wrote his book as a protest against the many innocent people that were being tried and executed for witchcraft. Among those being picked up for consorting with the devil were street magicians. Scot apologized for having to reveal the secrets of their tricks but said that it was purely

to show that they'd nothing to do with the supernatural.

What's amazing is that if we look at the tricks in Scot's book, we can see that they are very similar to the tricks the television magicians perform today. He describes tricks in which coins vanish from one hand and appear in the other, change value and penetrate a tabletop. There are even card tricks – how to find a selected card, how to "force" a card and how to change four Jacks into four aces.

Many magicians and mind-readers today dress their tricks up as "psychological illusion". They claim to be able to discover thoughts by studying your body language. This technique was described by Scot as long ago as the sixteenth century in a trick in which the performer correctly guesses which of three cards the spectator's thinking of.

David Blaine cut off his ear and ripped out his heart on television but in the Middle Ages magicians were always stabbing themselves, cutting off their noses and even the heads of their assistants. Once on air I used a large knife to apparently sever the arms of several "volunteers" in the Old Square in Prague. A version of a very similar trick is described in Scot's *Discoverie of Witchcraft*. The biblical quotation "there is nothing new under the sun" is particularly apt with regard to the world of magic.

Max Malini

There have been many great characters throughout the history of magic and one of the best was Max Malini. He was born in Poland in 1873 and migrated to the United States with his family when very young, serving his apprenticeship in the trade of the tricks in the rough bars of New York's Bowery. He was a short, squat man, with small hands and a guttural accent. His manners apparently left a lot to be desired and he mangled the English language badly. His audiences put it down to European eccentricity, enduring his less than polished etiquette because his magic was simply astounding.

From humble beginnings Malini was soon making fortunes entertaining at elite social gatherings. When he turned up at a fancy house to entertain a ballroom full of guests, the host would often be concerned that Malini appeared to have no equipment with him. "Where are your illusions, your assistants?" they'd ask. Malini would reply, "I am the show." And he'd prove to be right. With just a deck of cards, a couple of cigars and a hat he could put on a performance of magic the like of which they'd never seen. It wasn't unusual for Malini to receive tips of several hundred dollars on top of his thousand-dollar fee. And this was in the 1920s. Often his

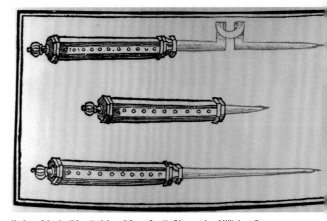

Various fake bodkins "prickers" from Scot's *Discoverie of Witchcraft*.

clients would give him gifts in appreciation of his performances; expensive jewellery such as rings and brooches. The King of Siam once gave him a jade pendant with the name Malini emblazoned across it in diamonds.

Like the television magicians of today, Malini was a great self-publicist. At a White House reception, he ripped the button off the coat of President Warren G. Harding. Harding was shocked until Malini magically restored the button to its rightful position. The shock turned to amazement and Malini managed to turn this simple little trick into front page news.

Malini is sometimes known as the last of the mountebanks, the dictionary definition of which is a flamboyant deceiver; someone who uses jokes and tricks to sell quack medicine to his audience. I think that he knew back then what we've only recently come to appreciate – that close-up or "street" magic is a very powerful and unique form of entertainment. There are many parallels between Malini and contemporary street magicians – he took his magic direct to the people, performing it with anything that came to hand and creating a sensation based not only on his tricks but with his larger-than-life personality. If television had been around in Malini's time there's no doubt that he'd have blagged his way into the producer's office and after performing a couple of tricks would have walked away with his own series. And probably the producer's watch too!

Modern Magic

In this book we'll take lessons learned from the street performers of the past to heart – this is street magic as in street-wise and savvy. In this book I've included some of the very best tricks that magic has to offer. You won't needs lots of cash to buy expensive props and there are no tricks with special boxes, brightly coloured silk handkerchiefs or feather flowers; we'll leave that stuff to the

A conman fleecing his victims with the Three Card Monte scam, c.1893.

Max Malini, hustler extraordinaire, from when top hats for magicians was a cool idea. Got to love his catchphrase: "I only cheat a little!"

progressively more demanding, not purely in terms of technical skill but also in terms of how you present each trick. We'll start with some very simple magic and then work our way through coins and cards to mind-reading and scams. As a general rule, you'll find that the last trick in each chapter is the most ambitious. It's designed to make the most of your skills and have maximum impact on your audience – these routines have pride of place in many professional magicians' repertoires. The goal of the book is to get you performing great magic as quickly as possible. Even if you only ever mastered the tricks in the first chapter, you'd still have an impressive arsenal ready for any occasion.

At this point I should apologize to all the left-handers reading this book because the photos and descriptions are from a right-handed person's perspective. You're going to have to reverse the right and left instructions unless you want to learn to do everything right-handedly. It shouldn't be too much of a problem though – I know because I've had to do that myself with every magic book I've read in the past thirty years – I'm actually left-handed. I just hope you appreciate how hard it was having to do all the tricks the other way round for the photos!

cruise ship performers. Instead it contains tricks using everyday objects that everyone can relate to – a deck of cards, a handful of coins, a pen and paper. Despite this, the tricks have the potential to be baffling and to get incredible reactions from the audience – I've seen people scream, laugh and even cry!

Quicker than the Eye?

There's a popular misconception that the hand is quicker than the eye. This is not actually the case; it's just one of the many myths surrounding the performance of magic. Many great tricks require almost no dexterity at all because magic tricks don't fool the eye – they fool the mind. When you perform a piece of magic you're really telling a story; one that leads the audience up the garden path to a surprise destination – you set up an expectation and then confound it. For the duration of the telling, the audience enter into an unspoken agreement with the performer to suspend their disbelief for a while. What your story does is help the audience to fool itself.

Some of the best tricks in this book are almost self-working. They have clever methods and anyone who can follow instructions will be able to master the mechanics of the trick quite quickly. I reckon that in less than a week you'll be able to perform at least half a dozen tricks from this book. Other tricks are more difficult and use some sleight-of-hand but once you've mastered them you'll have a skill for life.

A Course in Magic

The chapters in this book are arranged so that the magic gets

Don't Repeat a Trick

Someone once said, "It's fun to be fooled but it's more fun to know." When you first get into magic that's certainly true. Magicians want to know the secret to every trick that they possibly can, whether they are going to perform them or not. They become intrigued with the whole world of deception and for magicians the methods behind the tricks can be as entertaining and interesting as the presentations. But this isn't true for the audience – once the audience knows how a trick is done, it loses interest. So no matter how much someone badgers you – "Oh go on, do it again!" – don't be tempted. The second time you do a trick you won't have the surprise element on your side and so you stand a good chance of getting busted. Show them a different trick, or one that starts out the same but has a twist in the plot and a different ending.

Secrets

Every trick has its secret and if you want to keep your reputation as a magician, you'd be stupid to give those secrets away. Once they know the secret of the trick, the spectators are not just disinterested – they're disappointed. Some of the best magic tricks have very simple secrets. The "Out of this World" card trick is a very good example of that; but the impact of the trick on the audience is awesome. The ending is so incredible that they truly believe, if only for a few moments, that there really is such a thing as Extra-Sensory Perception. If you explained the trick to them they'd feel cheated – you'd rob them of the magic that you've just created. Also, people generally only appreciate knowledge that they've had

Super smooth Italian–American trickster Tony Slydini...

to work to gain – if you give something away for nothing, then that's what it will appear to be worth.

The Real Secret

The way a trick works though is not the real secret of successful magic. The real secret is the way you put that trick across to your audience. How you present your magic will determine the way your audience will react. Think about a joke – you could write it down and get five people to read it out but only one might make it funny – it's down to the delivery. Similarly, unless you're a musician yourself, you wouldn't enjoy listening to a piece of music just because you knew that it was hard to play; you'd only enjoy it if it moved you in some way or the performance of it was entertaining.

There's an old showbiz saying, "If they like you, they'll like your act," and it's as true now as it ever was – people would rather watch someone they liked than someone who was just "clever". A good magician isn't just someone who knows a lot of secrets; a good magician is a performer. Someone who's able to make their audience feel good rather than stupid – people like to be entertained rather than fooled.

Your Magic

Throughout the book I've suggested lines and stories that hook the spectator into the trick and make them interested in the outcome of your actions. Never insist on showing tricks to people who really aren't interested. Instead, just perform a trick or two here and there when the time is right, let your skills speak for themselves then back off. If you're any good at all, your reputation as a magician will spread by word of mouth and people will soon be begging you to show them some magic. Don't give in too readily though – play a little hard to get! Every time you perform your tricks you want it to be a special occasion which will be remembered.

In the descriptions of the tricks, you'll see that I've outlined the kind of things you might say as you perform them. Magicians call this talk "patter". You should use it as a guide when learning a new trick but as soon as you're comfortable with the mechanics of the trick, you should think about changing the patter and making the routine more "you".

This brings us to the question of personality. There's a temptation for beginners to copy the style of people they see and admire on television. We all have a natural tendency to emulate

... Sly by name and sly by nature, he cashed in on his natural charm.

those who're successful, but you should be wary of copying their presentation too closely; it's going to look very odd to everyone when you get asked to do a trick and suddenly change your usual personality for a "borrowed" one.

There was a famous magician called Tony Slydini. He was superb at close-up magic; in fact he used to make a speciality out of one of the tricks in this book (Over Their Head). He had a very distinctive personality, he was small, smartly dressed, performed with very graceful mannerisms and talked with a heavy Italian accent that gave him a unique charm. He gave lectures to other magicians in which he described the workings of some of his tricks. I remember seeing a performance by someone who'd been to one of those lectures; a down-to-earth guy from the north of England. He was very good at magic but when he performed one of Slydini's routines he suddenly took on a fake Italian accent. He even moved like Slydini, making graceful gestures in the air with his podgy hands. He wasn't just doing one of Slydini's tricks; it was as if he'd been possessed by him. It looked ridiculous, more like bad comic-acting than magic, and yet when he was being himself his magic was faultless; a perfect combination of skill and his natural personality.

The best persona to adopt when performing magic is your own. Ironic as it might seem, this is one of the hardest things to do! Think about the kind of person you are and how other people perceive you – don't be afraid to ask close friends the traits that they associate with you. And then try to think objectively about the kind of magic the person they describe might do and how they'd present it.

Final Thoughts

Magic's come a long way since street magicians were tried for

witchcraft and it's survived competition from all the other entertainments and technological marvels that have battled for the world's attention. This may be partly because everyone craves a little escapism from their daily routine and magic can momentarily provide that without having to rely on the trappings of technology or conventional entertainment venues – magic can happen at the most unexpected moment in the most unlikely of settings, reminding you that things aren't necessarily quite as they seem. Whatever the reason, magic will always be around in one form or another and by studying this book you can be a part of its future. You never know – one day you might even end up with your own TV show!

Practice hard, be yourself, concentrate on the presentation but above all else – have fun!

Paul Zenon

American magician David Blaine under-dressed for standing inside a block of ice, 2000. Some people will do anything rather than learn a couple of jokes.

Yours truly with René Lavand, legendary Argentinian magician. One of the world's greatest sleight-of-hand experts, despite only having one hand.

Chapter one
AUTO-MAGIC

Time to learn some magic so let's start with something easy. The tricks in this chapter are designed to give you a taste of what it's like to be a magician. They're virtually self-working so you don't have to worry about carrying out complicated moves – you can devote all your effort to making the routine as entertaining as possible. Learn a couple of them and try them out on your friends. Be warned though – applause and admiration can be addictive!

THREE-CUP MONTE

You had an accident when you were a child. You banged your head when you fell downstairs and ever since then you've had a kind of heightened intuition: at least, that's what you've been telling your spectators. The accident left you with strange psychic powers and you're now about to demonstrate them.

You take three cups and you borrow a small personal object from one of the spectators. While your back is turned they place it under one of the cups and then move a couple of them around to further confuse you. However, using your special psychic gift you can turn around and lift the correct cup to reveal the hidden object.

You can use any three cups for this, from your best china to disposable cardboard ones. The only bit of preparation is that one of the cups must be subtly marked so that you can distinguish it from the other two. It can be a slight flaw in the china, a pencil mark, a dent or nail nick in the cardboard; not something glaringly obvious, as shown in the photos, but something tiny only you will notice. With that in mind, here are the rest of the instructions:

Lay the cups, mouth-down, in a line on the table and note the position of your marked cup. Let's assume it's the middle cup of the three **(1)**. Turn your back and ask one of the spectators to take out some personal object which will fit under the cup. They can use a ring or lipstick or cigarette lighter or roll a banknote into a ball; anything that will fit. Tell them to place the object secretly under one of the cups. Tell them to confuse matters a little further by switching the positions of the two empty cups. Chances are you'll hear them do this, but ask them to tell you when they've finished anyway. Then turn around to face the cups and the spectators. Extend your hands and rub them together as if generating some kind of static electricity. You aren't: it just looks vaguely mysterious and makes the audience think the way the trick works has something to do with this.

Ask the spectator who loaned the object to identify themselves and, as soon as they step forward, extend one of your hands and touch him or her. Again, this has absolutely nothing to do with the trick but it'll make what you do next look more magical.

Keep your hand extended and move it over the cups. Pretend that you're feeling for some kind of psychic vibrations. What you're really doing is looking for your marked cup, because the position of that cup will reveal the position of the object. You know that the marked cup started in the middle. If it's still there, you know that the object is underneath it. That's because the spectators were asked to switch the

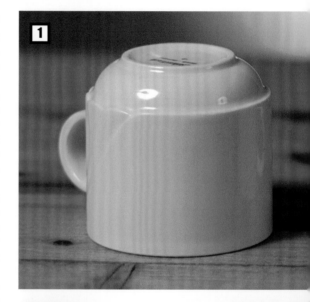

two cups that were not covering the object. If the marked cup is on the right, though, it means the object must be under the cup on the left **(2).** Conversely, if the marked cup is on the left, then the object must be under the cup on the right **(3)**. Think about it and you'll see how a marked cup and some simple instructions can reveal the object's position. Next comes the important phase; revelation. Build it up. Don't just lift the correct cup; that makes it look too easy. Pause a while and stare into their eyes; look as if you really are picking up psychic vibrations. Keep the spectators in suspense and finally, say, "It seems to be this one" and lift the correct cup. Do it right, and they will believe that you have extraordinary powers.

NOTE: This trick bears repeating. It's worth adding a few lines of bogus explanation when asking for an object, too: for example, "It doesn't work with anything made of rubber – but metal, plastic and paper are fine." It takes the audience's mind away from the real method and makes them think that perhaps there really is something special about your mental powers after all. And remember; the marked cup doesn't have to start in the middle. As long as you know the starting position of the marked cup you can use logic to work out the position of the object. This means that you can let them arrange the cups on the table. The less you touch the cups, the more impressive the trick will be.

EAR TODAY

A comical trick with a coin and a pen. You say you're going to make the coin disappear. You hit it three times with the pen, but instead of the coin disappearing, the pen does. Where did it go? You turn your head to reveal that it hasn't actually vanished at all – it's tucked behind your ear. When you draw their attention back to the coin, though, this time it really has disappeared.

This trick is all about timing and a widely-used principle in magic called "misdirection". It works because while the audience is keeping a keen eye on the coin, you're busy sneaking the pen away. And then, when their attention is focused on the pen, you secretly get rid of the coin. That's basically what misdirection is all about; diverting the audience's attention to where you want it rather than where it might naturally be, thereby allowing you to carry out all manner of sneaky moves.

Take out a coin and place it on your left palm. "Let me show you this – it's not quite ready, but I think I've got the hang of it – it's the vanishing coin trick." You then take a pen from your pocket in readiness to use it as a low-rent magic wand **(1)**. "You just tap the coin three times with the pen and it completely disappears – watch." Stand with your left side angled slightly toward the audience. Raise your right hand high, bending it at the elbow and then bring the pen down to hit the coin, counting "One". Do the same again, counting "Two." **(2)** As you raise the pen a third time, you shove it behind your ear **(3)** and, without breaking the stride, count "Three", bringing your empty right hand down as if to hit the coin again. Do a comedy double-take as you suddenly notice that the pen isn't there any more **(4)**. "Hang on – I think I got it the wrong way round: maybe it's the pen that was supposed to

3

5

disappear!" Give it a moment for them to register that the pen's gone and then say, "Actually, some of you might have spotted how I did that!" Turn your head round slowly and point out the pen wedged behind your ear **(5)**.

This should get a laugh from the audience, thinking that the whole thing's just a gag rather than an actual trick. That's your misdirection, though: as you remove the pen from behind your ear, your left hand secretly drops the coin into your left pocket which is covered by your body. As soon as you've ditched it, your left hand returns to the palm-up position as you turn back round. Hold the left hand as if it's still holding the coin, but with the fingers slightly curled

6

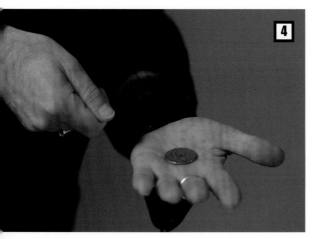

4

so that the audience can't see that it's not actually there any more. "But the weird thing is, when the pen comes back... that's when the coin actually goes!" Tap your left fingers with the pen and slowly open them to reveal that the coin has indeed disappeared **(6)**.

NOTES

The method for this trick is very simple, but it's a great quickie if you play it well and it doesn't require any preparation. It takes a knack to get the timing right on the upward swings of the right hand so that when you leave the pen behind your ear you don't break the rhythm. The reason no one sees the pen go is because their attention is centred exclusively on the coin in your left hand; you've told them that the coin will disappear and they're intent on seeing that happen. It's amazing how people will miss anything that happens outside their own small circle of focus. ✋

ANTI-GRAVITY CARDS

In this trick, you appear to make playing cards cling to the palm of your hand as if they're magnetized.

To do this trick you need a small blob of stationery adhesive (Blu-Tac or similar) hidden in your right hand. It's pressed against the middle finger and concealed **(1)**. You also need a deck of playing cards. Begin by shuffling your feet on the floor as if building up static electricity. Tell the spectators, "This isn't really magic; it's something most people can do – unless you're wearing rubber soles. It doesn't work with rubber soles." This is a lie, but all part of the psychological build-up. Ask someone to count off ten playing cards from the deck on to your palm-up left hand. The counting proves that the cards are unprepared. Push off the top card on to the right fingers **(2)**.

Press the card against the adhesive and then hold the right

hand out flat, palm-upwards. It looks as if the card is simply lying on the open hand. Shuffle one of your feet against the floor as if trying to build up a little more static. Trust me: this is the kind of bizarre behaviour that will make them think it's genuine. Start to slide the ten cards, one at a time, between that first card and your hand in a fairly even but random-looking fashion around it **(3)**. Continue sliding cards into position until they're all used up **(4)**.

You now have a platter of cards balanced on your hand. Place your left hand on top of the right, sandwiching all the cards. Extend your arms and, still holding the cards between your hands, slowly turn the

cards upside-down **(5)**. "Okay; let's try it," you say. And slowly you take your left hand away – all the cards appear to cling to your hand **(6)**.

It looks pretty weird – let everyone get a good look at the cards so that they can appreciate what's happened. Then walk up to someone, saying, "This is the bit that hurts – me, not you." Slowly touch that person on the shoulder. Having watched you generate all that static he'll be worried about what's going to happen. As soon as you touch him, yell out in pain. Immediately curl the fingers of your right hand and let all the cards fall to the floor. It looks as if you have suddenly discharged all the static electricity that was holding them in place. Shake the last card free, if necessary, shouting, "Ow! Ow! I hate that bit!"

Clutching your right hand as if you've been electrocuted, you'll have plenty of cover to steal away the blob of adhesive with your left hand and then later drop it into your pocket. Hold out your right hand for examination, saying, "Sometimes I get a blister." Fortunately, on this occasion you won't. People will want to examine the cards and try for themselves. It won't be long before someone is shuffling their feet against the carpet trying to build up enough static.

NOTES

Any kind of adhesive can be used for this trick, even chewing gum, which is very easy to rid of – just pop it back into your mouth as you kiss your imaginary blister better!

ON A ROLL

All you need for this trick is a pair of ordinary dice. Anyone can roll the dice and add up the top and the bottom numbers of each and you can immediately tell them what the total is. Sounds unbelievable but it's totally self-working. Once you understand the principle that makes it work you'll be able to devise your own presentations.

Start by handing the dice to a spectator. Ask her to roll them a couple of times so she's sure they're not loaded, they're just ordinary dice. Now take off your watch, telling the spectators you're going to make a prediction. The key number in this routine is 14. That's the number you're going to set on your watch.

If you have a watch with hands, set the minute hand to 1 and the hour hand to 4. If you have a digital watch, set it to 00.13, which gives you a minute to do the rest of the trick before the time changes to 00.14. Don't reveal your prediction to the spectators yet. Just place your watch face-down on someone's palm and get them to put their other hand on top so that no one can get at it.

Now turn to the spectator with the dice and say, "This time I want you to roll the dice for real and we're going to use the top and bottom numbers. Okay – roll 'em." When the dice come to a stop, ask the spectator to add up the two top numbers and call out the total. When that's done ask them to turn one of the dice completely over and add the bottom number. And when they've done that, ask them to turn over the second dice and add that bottom number too.

As long as they've followed your instructions, they'll always arrive at a total of 14. "Fourteen," you say, "that's strange – take a look at my watch. What numbers are the hands set at?" They should be amazed to find that the hands are set at 1 and 4.

NOTES

This trick works because the top and bottom numbers of all dice always add up to 7. And because we're using two dice the totals add up to 2 x 7, which is 14. You can make the prediction in many different ways; instead of using your watch, you could just write it down, but the more dramatic you make the revelation, the better.

Here's one way that will really freak people out. Just before you do the trick, roll up your left sleeve and use your fingernail to lightly scratch the number 14 on your forearm. Just a light scratch; don't do yourself any real damage! The scratch will show up as white, but will quickly disappear. Not long after you've done this, you give the spectator the dice and ask her to roll them and add up the top and bottom totals as described. She arrives at the number 14. You take the dice in your left hand and squeeze them hard. "Fourteen," you say, "let me try this."

Give the dice another squeeze and then roll up your left sleeve, transfer the dice to your right hand and start to rub your forearm with them. Incredibly, the number 14 will now appear in red on your arm. It looks really weird. Alternatively, you can write the number on your forearm with the edge of a bar of wet soap. Once it's dried, it will be invisible. Get the spectator to add up the total from the dice and write it on a piece of paper in secret, then burn it in an ashtray. Take the ashes and rub them on your arm to make the number 14 appear in black. Spooky.

SORCERER'S APPRENTICE

Once you get a reputation as a magician, people will start asking you to teach them a trick. It's difficult to refuse. On the other hand, you don't actually want to start giving your tricks away. This routine is a good compromise – you turn the spectator into the magician.

You choose a card and they find it. Yet they're completely baffled as to how they did it. Having been pestered to teach a trick, you hand the spectator a deck of cards, saying, "Okay, try this – you'll be the magician and I'll be the spectator. Here: take the deck and give it a shuffle."

As he shuffles, offer him a few compliments on his technique. "That's slick. I think you're going to be good at this." Then stop him shuffling the cards and tell him it's time you took a card. "I'll take a card and you'll be able to tell me what it is. Sound good?" Sounds too good to be true. He has no idea how you can make good on this promise.

Get him to hold the cards up towards you and spread them so that you can see the faces. Pretend to be a difficult customer, saying, "Let me try to pick a difficult card. This'll get ya!"

What you're actually doing is spreading through the cards so that you can get a good look at the two top cards of the deck. Let's assume they're the eight of hearts and the King of spades. You'll cross-reference these two cards to lead you to a third card. For instance, if you mix the numbers and suits of the two examples here you could arrive at either the King of

hearts or the eight of spades. Either card will work for this trick, so simply look through the deck until you find either of them and then take it out. Let's assume you take out the eight of spades. Put it face-down on the table, saying, "Perfect. You'll never guess this – unless you're really a magician. Let's see."

Tell the spectator to square up the cards again. Remember the two cards you spotted earlier will be on top of the deck. Now ask him to deal cards face-down one at a time into a pile on the table. "Off you go; start dealing." As he's dealing, you say to him, "Now, a real magician would know exactly when to stop. Do you know when to stop?" He'll probably admit that he has no idea. So just tell him, "Stop dealing any time you like. You're the magician – your decision."

At some point the spectator will stop dealing cards on to the table. Tell him to put the rest of the cards away for the moment. Then ask him to square up the pile on the table and pick it up. "Okay: nearly there. Now all you've got to do is deal the cards alternately into two piles. Off you go, Magic Boy." Make sure he follows your instructions properly, dealing one card to the right and then one to the left and so on until he has no cards left in his hand. Now,

if you've been following this closely you'll realize that the top cards of the two piles are now the same cards you noted earlier – the eight of hearts and the King of spades.

Here's how you use that information. Ask him to turn over the top card of one of the piles. Let's assume it's the eight of hearts. Now, this is the same value as the card you placed face-down on the table, so ask the spectator, "What value is that card?" He'll say "Eight." Tell him to turn over the top card of the other pile, the King of spades. This is the same suit as the card

you placed on the table so ask him, "And what suit is that?" He'll answer "Spades." Point to the eight of hearts and ask him again for its value. Then point to the King of spades and ask him for its suit.

Keep doing this so that he's constantly repeating the words, "Eight, spades, eight, spades." Finally point to the face-down card you placed on the table and say, "And what card do you think I took earlier?" He'll inevitably say, "Eight of spades." Turn up the card and show that he's correct. Then turn to him and say,

"That's the best I've ever seen it done. But please, don't tell anyone how you did it – it's our little secret."

NOTES

The only time this trick won't work is if the two top cards are the same value or suit: for example, a Queen of hearts and Queen of clubs or a six of hearts and a nine of hearts. To get around this, just take one of those cards, look at it for a moment and then push it back into the middle of the deck, saying, "Nah: way too easy. Let me take another one." You can do this as many times as you like: it's all part of the fun of you playing the role of the awkward spectator. ✍

Chapter two
THE MIDAS TOUCH

Ready for something tougher? Tricks with money always go down well and in this chapter you'll learn some classics. There are hundreds of tricks with coins and the reason is that they're great things to manipulate – they can be palmed, vanished and produced very easily.

I've described some of the basic building blocks of sleight-of-hand magic in this chapter. Learn these well and you'll be ready for more advanced tricks with all kinds of objects.

THE CLASSIC PALM

This is one of the most fundamental and important moves in coin magic. It's called palming and allows you to hide a coin in your hand without anyone being aware of it.

Let's take a look at the secret position the coin will be held in. It's gripped by the muscles at the base of the thumb on one side and the fleshy part of the palm on the other **(1)**. It takes a lot of practice to hold the coin there comfortably, but when it's held properly you can turn the hand completely over and the coin won't fall free **(2)**. Although you have a coin palmed in your hand, you're still able to pick up other objects with your thumb and fingers **(3)**.

You can even wiggle or snap your fingers. Still being able to use

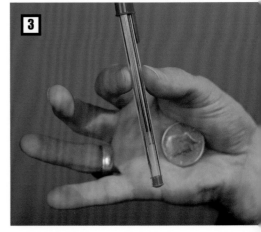

the hand for other actions while palming is what makes it so deceptive. To get the coin into the correct position, start with it on the tips of the right fingers **(4)**. Using the middle finger, push the coin along the underside of the thumb **(5)**.

If you push it far enough, the coin will automatically finish at the correct position for palming **(6)**. Getting the coin from the fingers to the classic palm only takes a second and it can be performed with the hand casually by your side or even in motion. You can even momentarily place your hand in your pocket, pick up a coin from your change and classic-palm it without the action being noticed by the audience.

NOTES

The classic palm is so fundamental to coin magic that I'd recommend you practice it at every available opportunity. Spend enough time on it and you'll discover that you can palm more than one coin at a time. T. Nelson Downs, an American magician who used to bill himself as The King of Koins (great magician, lousy speller!), could palm a dozen or more silver dollars with ease. Now that's dedication.

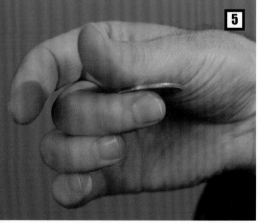

THE FRENCH DROP

Time for your first sleight-of-hand coin trick. It uses a move known as the French Drop, and it can be used to make a coin disappear. It looks as if you take a coin in your left hand and then close your fingers around it. You blow on the hand, open the fingers and the coin has gone.

Begin by taking a coin out of your pocket and then holding it at the tips of the right fingers and thumb **(1)**.

The position of the right hand and the coin is very important. The fingers are below the coin and the thumb on top. And the coin is held with the flat side facing the spectators.

As you hold the coin, make some casual comment, "This will work with any coin, but the newer the better – it's to do with the copper content." Pure bull, but it gets the spectators intrigued as to what on earth you're going to do. The left hand comes over the coin **(2)**, and the coin is apparently taken away **(3)**. This is where ☞

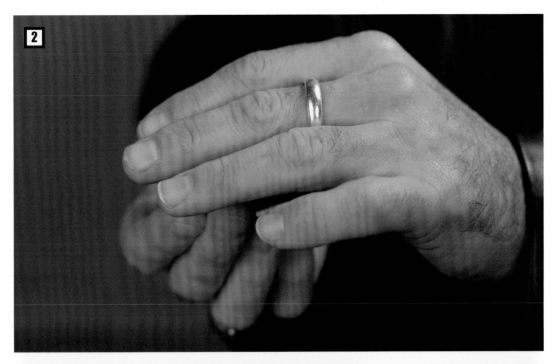

the French Drop takes place, however, because as soon as the coin was hidden behind the left fingers, it dropped on to the right fingers **(4)**. The photo shows the performer's point of view.

Now close the left fingers and thumb as if actually taking the coin and move the hand away to the left. Spectators will see an empty space between the right fingers and thumb where the coin used to be. In fact the coin is hidden from their view by the curve of your right fingers **(5)**.

You will find that the coin can be held securely and comfortably in the curled fingers of the right hand. This is known as the "finger palm". Continue moving the left hand to the left, closing it slightly as if it's holding the coin. As you do this, casually let the right hand and its finger-palmed coin fall by your right side.

It's a tried and tested rule of magic that wherever you look, the spectators will tend to look. You're able to direct the attention of the spectators to any area you choose while performing tricks, so if you look at the left hand as it moves to the left, the spectators will usually look at that hand too. And by drawing attention to the left hand, you're also drawing attention away from the guilty right hand.

Following up your earlier remark about copper content, say, "And the odd thing is that if you apply a little friction to warm it up, like this, something strange happens." Rub the fingers of the left hand together as if applying friction to the coin. At the same time, you Classic Palm the coin that's in the right hand.

Here's a reminder: as your right hand hangs by your side, let the coin fall to the fingertips. Now with the right middle finger, push the coin upwards along the underside of the thumb until it reaches the palm. Keep pushing the coin until it can be held between the thumb muscle on one side and the fleshy part of the palm on the other.

From the spectators' point of view, it doesn't look as if there could now be any coin hidden in the right hand. Okay: back to the trick. Finish pretending to rub the coin and then extend your left hand. With your right hand, reach up and grasp the left sleeve at the elbow. Pull the sleeve back as you say, "Watch." Squeeze the fingers of your left hand together as if crushing the coin and then one by one open them to reveal that the coin has completely disappeared. The trick is over: the coin has apparently been

4

5

crushed into nothingness.

However, this does leave you with a coin palmed in the right hand, which is never a good position to be in. Don't be in a hurry to get rid of the evidence, though: as the saying goes, there's no need to run if no one is chasing you. There's no bigger giveaway than seeing a magician immediately go to his pockets after something has disappeared. Don't be afraid of keeping the coin palmed: as far as the audience is aware, it's gone and the trick's over.

If you don't act guilty, the spectators will have no reason to assume that you are. Move on to your next trick and ditch the coin in your pocket when the heat is off.

NOTES

The biggest hurdle in this trick is not the mechanics of the French Drop: it's the ability to make the moves smooth and natural. Always keep in mind what you're supposed to be doing – simply taking a coin from the right hand in the left hand prior to making it disappear.

A good tip is actually to take the coin in the left hand for real several times and study what the movements look like before trying to copy them using the move. If you're wearing a shirt or jacket with a breast pocket, you can actually get rid of the coin completely. When you pull your left sleeve back, allow the right hand to come right over the opening of the breast pocket. You'll find that from this position you can drop the coin from the palm position directly into the pocket.

At the end of the trick, both hands are completely empty. Make sure that the pocket is empty at the start of the trick. You don't want to give the game away by someone hearing the coin clink against something inside as it drops.

Another way of getting rid of the need to ditch the palmed coin is to reproduce it. You can use that old standby of pretending to reach out and pluck it from behind a spectator's ear. To do this, you first direct the spectators' attention to someone in the audience by looking at them, saying, "What's that there?"

As you stare at their ear, relax your body, allow your right hand to fall by your side and the coin to fall on to the fingers. Then reach up behind the person's head and as you do, use your thumb to push the coin to the fingertips. As they ask, "What?" you reply "This 'ere!" and pull your hand back as if really pulling the coin from their ear. The better your acting at this point, the better the effect on the audience.

It's an old trick but it still goes down well, particularly with children. Another comical finish is to produce the coin from your nose. Reach up with the right hand and grasp the bridge of your nose between the right fingers and thumb. The left hand is held palm-up at chest height below the nose. Make a nose-blowing sound and then let the coin fall from the right palm on to the left hand. From the front, it looks exactly as if it's been snorted out of your nose!

CAP IN HAND

When you've mastered the French Drop, you can progress to this little baffler. You take a coin and tap it with a pen. The coin then disappears. You take the cap off the pen and then apparently shake the coin out of it. It's a quick magical sequence which looks absolutely impossible.

Let's assume that the pen is in your breast pocket, where it can be easily reached with your left hand. Borrow a coin and hold it at the right fingertips in position for the French Drop **(1)**. Say, "This coin's very deceptive. Looks solid, but watch this..." Apparently take the coin in the left hand, but actually execute the French Drop **(2, 3)**.

NOTES

Once you understand the handling of the trick, you can choreograph it to suit yourself. The main thing to learn is to be open and easy with the moves. If working over a table, then allow the coin to drop on to it when it reappears: but if you're standing when you perform you might ask a spectator to hold out their hand before you remove the cap from the pen. Then give it a shake and let the coin fall on to their palm for a surprise finish.

Take out the pen with the right hand and use it as a wand to tap the left hand. Open the left hand to show that the coin has disappeared **(4)**. The coin is actually finger-palmed in the right hand. Tell the spectators, "Looks as if the coin has disappeared, but actually – you're not going to believe this – it's inside the pen!" This clearly doesn't make much sense because there's no way the coin can fit within the diameter of the pen.

Nevertheless, make a play of handling the pen so that the spectators truly believe that your hands are otherwise empty. Reposition the pen so that the right hand can pull the cap off **(5)**. Don't worry: the coin palmed in your right hand will be hidden from the audience. Remove the cap from the pen. Now bring the cap to a vertical position and give it a couple of sharp shakes as if trying to dislodge something from inside. On the final one, allow the palmed coin to fall from your hand, saying, "There it is!"

Done on the downswing, it appears as if the coin has suddenly popped out of the pen cap **(6)**: clearly an impossibility. All you need to do now is pocket your pen and hand the coin back to the spectator.

THE GREAT ESCAPE

A large silver coin is folded up inside a square of paper. The coin can be clearly seen through a small hole in the paper packet. It really is there: and yet, with a flick the coin visibly jumps right through the small hole, penetrating the wall of its paper prison. This is a genuinely stunning illusion.

The optical illusion which makes this trick work was discovered by Bob Ostin, a very creative magician from Liverpool. The version described here has been simplified to put it within the abilities of those starting out in magic. You'll need one large silver coin. It doesn't need to be huge, but it needs to be a fairly heavy one for it to work properly. Because of the optical illusion involved in the trick, silver works better than copper. You'll also need a square of paper. It should be just over three times larger than the diameter of the coin on all sides.

Fold it into thirds along its length and breadth until you have nine squares, each of which will comfortably take the coin you're using. Fold the paper into thirds and, with a hole punch, create a small hole right through the folded paper. Alternatively, you could cut a square hole using a craft knife.

When you open the paper, you'll have holes through three of the squares **(1)**. That's all the preparation you need. To perform, hand the coin out for inspection, especially if you're using a coin which isn't in common circulation. Then display the paper. "This coin represents Houdini," you say, "and this paper is his prison." You needn't present the story too seriously. Open the paper and place the coin on the centre square **(2)**. Raise the paper towards the spectators so that they can see the coin through the hole in the middle **(3)**. ☞

1

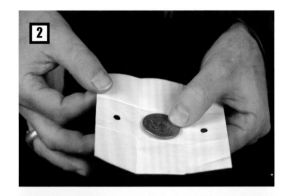

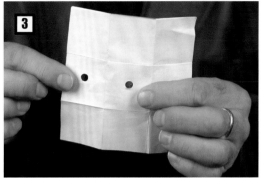

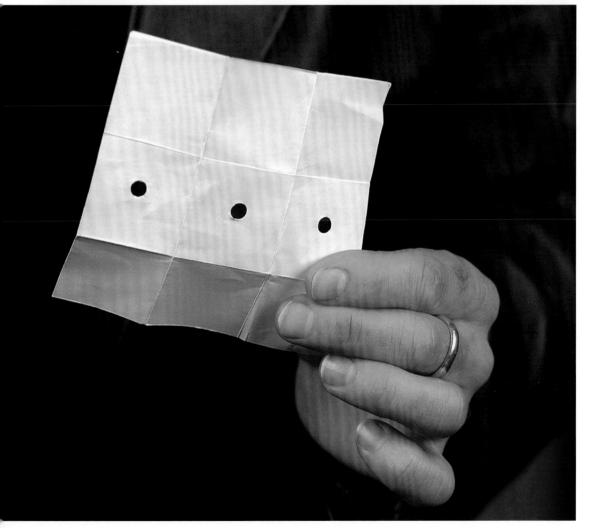

Your left thumb is on top of the coin. The right hand now folds the right hand side of the paper over the coin. But as it does so, two things happen. The first is that the right fingers cover the hole at the front so that the spectators can't see the coin. The second thing is that the left thumb pulls the coin to the left **(4)**. The photo shows your viewpoint. And as soon as the right side of the paper is folded,

the left thumb pushes the coin back to the right.

The result is that the coin is now above the folded right side of the paper **(5)**. The right thumb now grips the coin as the left hand folds the left side of the paper over it. The top third of the paper is now folded down behind the package, followed by the bottom third of the paper. The result is a small package of paper at the fingertips,

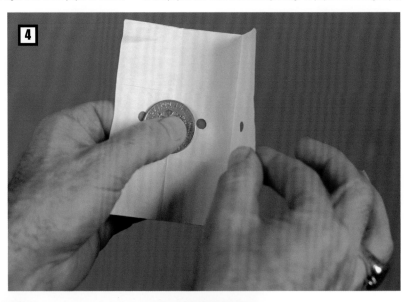

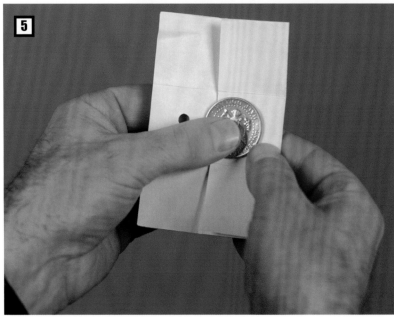

inside which is the silver coin **(6)**.

As far as the spectators are concerned, the coin is genuinely trapped within the folded package. They can still see it through the hole in the front. In fact, the coin isn't as secure as they imagine: it can actually slide out of the side on your right. But you don't want to slide the coin free just yet. To do that, you use the illusion Bob Ostin discovered. The left hand grips the upper left corner of the package between the thumb and forefinger, and the right forefinger is bent backwards ready to give the packet a hefty flick **(7)**.

Tell spectators, "They used to say that no prison cell could hold Houdini. He could always escape. Money's got a similar way with me. Watch the coin through the window." Flick the packet. What happens is that the impact shoots the coin out towards the spectators **(8)**.

It actually comes out of the right open side of the packet but so quickly that to the spectators it looks as if the coin has jumped right through the small hole. You'll have to try this in front of a mirror before you can appreciate how effective the illusion is.

NOTES

If you go through the moves slowly you'll see that the coin is out of the spectators' view for a brief time while you set it in the working position. No one will notice this because you haven't even told them to pay attention to the holes in the paper. Only mention them after the coin is set and ready to go. You might want to have the coin signed by a spectator with a marker pen. That way, when the coin jumps free they can check that it really is the same coin. As they do that, you can tear up the paper packet to prove that there is only one coin being used. Destroying the paper prevents anyone else trying the trick for themselves. Sneaky, huh?

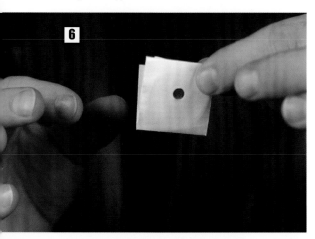

SNAPSHOT

This is a really cool vanish of a coin. You hold the coin at your fingertips, give it a squeeze and it completely disappears. Best of all, the method is as clever and straightforward as the effect.

The only drawback to this trick is that you need to be wearing a jacket when you perform it – but then it's about time you smartened yourself up! The reason you need a jacket is because you're going to shoot the coin up your sleeve. Everyone thinks magicians hide things up their sleeves and this is one of the few instances when you do! To make it easier, if you're wearing a long-sleeved shirt you should roll the sleeves up. It'll allow the coin an easier passage. Start by borrowing a coin from someone and then holding it up between the thumb and middle finger of your right hand so that everyone can see it **(1)**.

The critical point is that your forearm should be parallel to the floor. In a moment, you're going to flick the coin into the jacket

3

sleeve, and if the forearm is tilted it will affect the trajectory. Notice, too, how the sleeve hangs down below the wrist forming an opening that the coin can enter. A secret tug at the sleeve before you perform this trick will ensure that it hangs loose in the right way.

Draw attention to the coin, saying, "Watch carefully. I'm going to give the coin a squeeze..." And as you do so, actually squeeze the coin until your thumb and middle finger snap together with the coin flipped into a horizontal position. It will be pinched between the thumb and finger and from the front will be completely hidden **(2)**.

To the audience, it already looks as if the coin has disappeared. In fact, the coin is just projecting behind your closed thumb and fingers **(3)**.

The photo shows a view from the back. Continue, saying, "...and it completely disappears." Now snap the middle finger against the thumb. This will result in the coin being flicked back towards the opening of the sleeve **(4)**. The photos shows the view from the back. And if you flick it hard enough it will continue shooting up the sleeve, along ☞

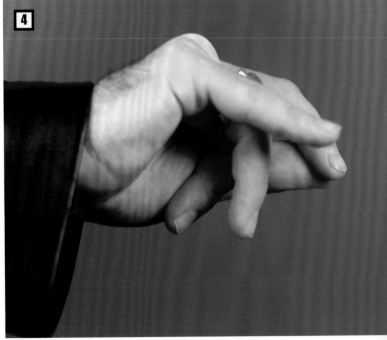

4

the arm and only stop when it reaches the elbow. As soon as the coin has gone, open the hand so that the empty palm is towards the spectators **(5)**.

Now they see that the coin really has disappeared. It's an instantaneous vanish. One moment the coin's there: the next moment it's gone. Turn to the man who loaned you the coin and say, "But the coin hasn't disappeared for ever. It's reappeared in your pocket – take a look."

He won't believe this and with good reason – it isn't true. However, as he searches through his pockets everyone will look at him. And if they're looking at him, they won't be looking at you. This gives you a chance to drop your right arm by your side and recover the sleeved coin. The coin will fall down your sleeve and drop into your cupped right fingers. From here you can classic-palm the coin. By this time the spectator will be telling you that the coin isn't in his pocket. "I didn't say it would stay there!" you continue, "It carried on over to here." Reach out and produce the coin from behind the next

spectator's ear as described earlier in this chapter. "I hope you weren't thinking of keeping that," you say, looking at him suspiciously, "Can't trust anyone these days!"

NOTES

This is probably not a sleight you'll master straight away. I recommend you practice with your back to a bed; that way you won't have far to bend every time the coin misses the sleeve! And you should make sure that you perform it while wearing the same jacket you rehearsed with. But it'll be worth the time spent, because it is very deceptive: it's as close to looking like real magic as you're likely to get.

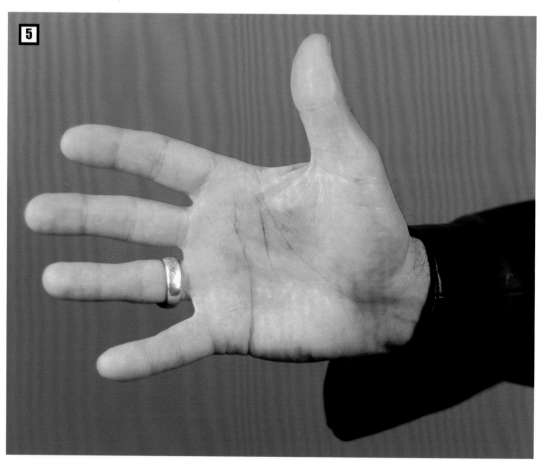

5

DEVALUED

You take a large coin and place it on your palm. You brush your other hand across it and instantly it changes into a smaller coin.

This instant and almost visible transformation once again makes use of sleeving. Begin by secretly classic-palming a small coin in your right hand, and then ask the spectators for the loan of a large coin. Say, apropos of nothing in particular, "It's amazing how quickly the value of money changes these days." Take the coin from the spectator with your right hand.

The right hand has the coin palmed, but the fact you're using

that hand helps persuade the spectators that both hands are empty at the beginning of this trick: so take the large coin in the right hand, but be careful not to reveal the palmed smaller one. Drop the large coin on to the palm-up left hand as you talk. The left hand is held just above waist height, which is the perfect position for the change which will follow. The right hand is held palm-down about six inches to the right **(1)**. ☞

1

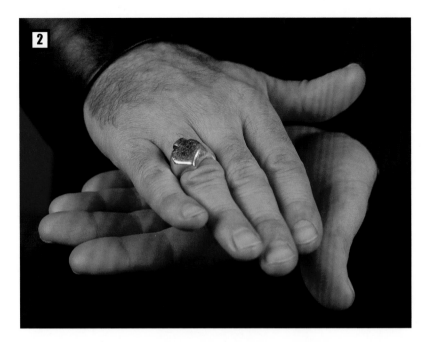

This is the starting position for the change. "Take a good look at that coin," you say. Now quickly move the left hand towards you, directly under the palm-down right hand. This will have the effect of propelling the large coin up the right sleeve **(2)**.

At the same time, you move the right hand forward, and as the large coin goes, let the palmed small coin fall on to the left hand. Move the hands apart and let the spectators see that the coin on the left palm has now apparently shrunk, all in the blink of an eye **(3)**.

Hand the coin to the spectator, saying, "Your money's not worth what it used to be, is it?" The change requires a lot of practice and good timing for it to work well.

When you first start to practice you'll probably exaggerate the movements in order to shoot the coin up the sleeve, but slowly you'll realize that very little movement is required. The hands just come together, the right hand barely covering the left palm for a second, and when they separate, the coin has changed.

NOTES

You can retrieve the sleeved coin as your left hand gives the samll coin to the spectator. Let the sleeved coin fall into the right hand and classic-palm it. Using the same moves you can now change the small coin into the large coin – which the spectator will more than likely insist on!

INFLATION

This is the natural follow-up to Devalued. You've just transformed a large coin into a small one. You now take the small coin back from the spectator, give it a rub with your fingers and, hey presto, it's now grown again.

This is simple to do and looks very magical. The small coin appears to change as the right fingers are rubbed across it (see photos **(1)**, **(2)** and **(3)**).

To perform this change, start with the large coin finger-palmed in your right hand. Take the small coin back from the spectator and hold it in your left hand, the "tails" side of the coin facing the spectators. The left thumb is on top of the coin and the fingers below **(4)**. The photo shows an exposed view. The position is very similar to the French Drop position you learned earlier. Say to the spectators, ☞

"Did you notice we started with the coin heads-up last time? Let me show you what happens when it's tails-up." Bring the right hand over the small coin **(5)**.

As soon as the coin is hidden from view, let it fall on to the left fingers. The finger-palmed large coin is now released so that it can be gripped with the left thumb on top and the left fingers below.

As soon as this exchange of coins has taken place, rub the right fingers on the large coin, saying, "Just warm it up a little and it starts to expand." Move the right hand away entirely, allowing the large coin into view **(6)**. Without making a big deal of it, casually turn your right hand over so that that the spectators can see that it's empty: to them, it looks as if you merely rubbed the small coin with your fingertips and it grew. Hand the coin back, Classic Palm the small coin in your left hand and ditch it at an appropriate moment.

NOTES

You don't have to stop with one coin change. I sometimes have a really big coin in my pocket. Find the most unusual and heaviest coin you can: a Chinese coin or medallion with a hole in it is perfect. As you ditch the small coin, pick up the extra-large coin and just hold it in the finger palm. Ask to see the spectator's coin again ("Sometimes they come back with a defect.") Position it ready for the move, and this time change the borrowed coin for the whopping hunk of metal that you have finger-palmed. When it's appeared, drop it on the table so that it lands with a clunk. The bigger the coin, the bigger the surprise on the spectators' faces will be. 🖐

JAZZING WITH COINS

Some of the best magic you'll ever do will be made up on the spur of the movement – jazz magic. Once you've mastered the coin sleights in this book, you'll be able to work miracles. All it requires is a little lateral thinking and the ability to spot an opportunity when it arises.

Learning New Skills

Let's review what you've learned so far. You can palm a coin, which means that you can also produce a coin, by plucking it from behind someone's ear or out of thin air. You can also vanish a coin using the French Drop or by shooting it up your sleeve. And you can change one coin into another. That's a good arsenal of magical weaponry, and with it you'll be able to blow a few people away.

Let's start by taking the classic palm. You've learned to palm one coin, but there's no reason you can't use exactly the same technique to palm two coins in the same hand. Three or four coins will require a bit more practice, but can be managed by most people after a while. By slowly easing the muscles of the hand, you'll find you can drop the coins from their palmed position one at a time. Learn to do this and you've immediately widened the scope of your magic. Learn to do it with both hands and you're a veritable sleight-of-hand expert.

The Art of Magical Improvisation

There's an old trick with the unlikely title of The Free and Unlimited Coinage of Silver. It was originally performed more than 100 years ago by a Viennese magician in a restaurant and it impressed the coin magic expert T Nelson Downs so much that he paid to learn the secret. It's as strong now as it was then.

Imagine you're sat down somewhere for a meal. It can be anywhere from McDonald's to the Ritz. There are cups and plates on the table and, unknown to your friends, you've got three identical coins palmed in your right hand. As you lift up your cup, move an ashtray or pick up a plate, you secretly release one of the palmed coins and quietly slip it under the object. Don't worry: no one will be paying any attention. You should have no difficulty in placing the coins: you're just setting the trick up as you eat your meal (obviously, don't put any coins under anything that your companions are likely to be picking up from the table).

When you finally get around to performing the trick, take out a matching fourth coin from your pocket. Ask someone to nominate one of the three objects on the table; unknown to them, there's a coin hidden underneath each. Then make the coin in your hand disappear using the French Drop. Ask the person to lift up the object that they chose. As they do, your right and left hands go to your pockets and palm several more coins.

The spectator will be amazed that the vanished coin has reappeared under the chosen object – but they won't be amazed for long. So you pre-empt their next thought by saying, "I know what you're thinking: there's a coin under the other two items as well. Let's see…"

You lift up one of the items to reveal a second coin, but as you put it down on the table, you load another coin from your palm under it. Lift up the third item with the other hand and reveal the third coin. Again, as you place the object back on the table, load another coin beneath it.

"It's a good job you didn't pick this one," you say as you lift up a plate and move it aside. As the plate is lifted, you allow one of the coins to drop from your palm on to the table. It looks as if the coin was under the plate all along. And as you set the plate down, load yet another coin beneath it. You can do this with several other objects, lifting them to find a coin underneath and then loading another coin under them as you place them back down.

The end result of this is that you've loaded all the palmed coins under all kinds of objects on the table. Pause, then say, "Let's do it again," and now, with your hands clearly empty, start picking up all the objects from the table to reveal even more coins beneath them. Scoop some of the coins up and drop them into your pocket – but secretly retain one, classic-palming it in the right hand.

A good way to finish the routine and produce the final coin is to pick up a folded paper napkin or beermat and rip it open to find the coin inside. Just fold it into four and press the coin up into the folds, then tear the centre out – it helps if you wet it – to apparently discover the coin embedded inside. With a little acting, you can make out that you are extracting the coin from the very centre. Similarly with a bread roll! ☞

You can also use the sleight which produced a coin from the pen cap in the Cap in Hand routine to shake a coin from a cigarette or blow it from a drinking straw. This routine is capable of many variations and you can improvise your way through it provided you've mastered some basic coin skills.

Rehearsed Spontaneity

The best magic arises out of natural situations. If you have to start every trick as if it's a formal performance, then people will be on their guard. They view what you do as a "show." Close-up or street magic should be more of a seemingly spontaneous "happening". That's why The Free and Unlimited Coinage of Silver works. After a meal, people are usually in a relaxed and happy frame of mind. The natural props you use – the cups, plates, ashtrays etc. – are already arranged in front of you and your audience, and your preparation for the trick has casually been done in secrecy. The magic, when it happens, is both unexpected and welcome.

To make this trick work in practice, though, you have to rehearse those moves well. You have to set up those same conditions at home with the table and all the items and practice until you can do the moves automatically, all the while making it look effortless. And you should be as surprised and pleased as the spectators are as each coin makes an appearance: enthusiasm is contagious.

The Three-Phase Routine

A structure which works well in magic as well as in other areas of performance is a routine which has three phases. The number three is a magical number. It might not be obvious, but The Free and Unlimited Coinage of Silver is a three-phase routine. In the first phase you make a coin disappear and appear under, say, a cup. In the second phase you reveal coins under every object on the table. And in the third phase you produce a coin from a totally impossible place, such as a bread roll. This three-part routine has a natural structure; it feels right in the same way that some jokes are funny because the structure and rhythm are right: in the same way that lists of three work well in speeches and the way that books and movies are usually best when written with the three essential components in mind – a beginning, middle and end. Use the unwritten rule of three to your advantage in your magic.

Here's an example of how to take two of the routines you've already learned and add a finish to form a three-phase routine. You produce a coin from nowhere, it penetrates a table and then transforms into a different coin entirely.

For this routine you're sitting down at a table and wearing your jacket so that you can do some sleeving. Earlier, you secretly put a large silver coin on your knee, and you have a smaller copper coin classic-palmed in your right hand.

When the opportunity arises, look at the table as you say, "What are all these bits on the table?" Stare at the table as if you mean it and pretend to be picking up little bits of dust off the table with your right hand and dropping them into your left hand, which is palm-up so that the spectators can see that it's empty. Keep the palm of your right hand towards you so that no one can see the palmed coin.

Gather some more imaginary dust and this time, as you apparently place it on the left palm, secretly drop the coin on to the left fingers. Close the left hand over the coin and turn it knuckle-side-up. You've now smuggled a coin into the left hand and, you hope, no one suspects a thing. Say, "If I squeeze tight, I might be able to show you something. Yep, that's it: done." Squeeze the left hand, snap the right fingers to accentuate the magic happening, and then open the hand and turn it over to reveal the copper coin. Take the coin in the right hand and tap it on the table to show that it is indeed a real, solid coin.

"That's weird," you say. "But this is even weirder..." Hold the coin in the right hand in readiness for the French Drop. Apparently take the coin in the left hand, actually palming it in the right.

Reach out with the left hand and tap the fingers (apparently still holding the coin) against the middle of the table. At the same time, your right hand goes below the table. While still holding the copper coin, it picks up and classic-palms the large silver coin.

Now press your left hand against the table-top as if trying to push the coin through. Immediately snap the copper coin against the underside of the table to create a noise to make it seem that you're pulling it right through the wood. Lift the left hand to show that the coin has disappeared. Bring the right hand from under the table and throw the copper coin on to the tabletop. "Bit strange, eh?"

You're ahead of the spectators because you still have a large silver coin classic-palmed in the right hand. Pick up the copper coin and put it on the open left palm in readiness for the Devalued move. Sleeve the copper coin and reveal the silver coin as you say, "And that's really strange!" Finish by tossing the silver coin on to the table. If you aren't wearing a jacket then use the change described in Inflation instead, and classic-palm the copper coin as you throw the silver one on to the table.

The Big Finish

Producing a big or unexpected object at the end of a routine makes for a nice finish. The techniques for classic-palming and the French Drop can be used with other objects such as dice, balled-up paper, sugar lumps, olives etc. You can buy giant-sized novelty coins at toy and magic shops; they make a great climax to any coin routine. Or produce something totally unexpected like an ice cube, or a rock that you can drop on to the table with a hefty thud. Ask yourself what would surprise you if a magician suddenly produced it, and then strive to find a way to make it possible. ✋

Chapter three
TOP SECRET GADGETS

Magicians have more gadgets than James Bond – dozens of special devices known as "gimmicks" that enable them to work miracles. The reason you use a gimmick is to enable you to perform a trick that would otherwise be impossible or extremely difficult to do by sleight-of-hand alone. In this chapter I've selected several that have stood the test of time – you'll have seen them used by street magicians and mind-readers in their TV shows.

DIGITAL DEXTERITY

You pick up a salt cellar and pour the contents into your closed left fist. A snap of the fingers, and all the salt disappears. But it doesn't go far – it reappears pouring in a stream from your right hand!

1

The trick is made possible through a secret gimmick magicians call a "thumb tip". It's a hollow fake thumb, flesh-coloured, usually made of plastic, and it fits over your real thumb. As you can see, they come in a variety of styles! **(1)**

They're sold in magic and novelty stores the world over. Don't worry too much about the colour matching your skin precisely; when it's used properly it's not really in view of the audience and you'll use movement as added camouflage. It should fit loosely so that you can get it on and off your thumb easily, with room inside for whatever you're making disappear or appear. It's one of the most versatile gimmicks ever devised for the magician and you'll find endless uses for it.

But first, let's learn how to use it to make a pile of salt disappear and then reappear.

Start with the thumb tip in your right pocket. The salt cellar is on the table in front of you. As you pick the salt cellar up in your left hand, put your right hand in your pocket and get the thumb tip in place on your right thumb. Don't be self-conscious about the weird-looking blob of plastic: if you don't pay attention to it, no one else will. Let's imagine you're in a café, standing up with the salt cellar in your left hand **(2)**. The photo shows your point of view.

You engage the spectators' attention with a bizarre story. "Have you ever seen people filling these salt cellars? Neither have I. You know why? They don't need to. The salt makes its way into the cellar all by itself. I'll show you what I mean." With your right hand, take the salt cellar from the left and, as you do, extend your right thumb so that it enters the left hand. Leave the thumb tip gripped and hidden in the left hand as you take the salt cellar away in the right **(3)**.

Tip the salt cellar slightly and pour out a little of the salt, letting it fall to the table or floor. This is just to show that it's real. As you do that, the fingers of the left hand close into a fist and position the thumb tip so that it's open end upwards, hidden in the hand. "I'll just use a little bit," you say as you openly pour the salt into the left hand and into the thumb tip **(4)**, letting the salt flow out in a long thin stream from a good height above it. You don't actually pour very much salt into the thumb tip at all, but if you pour it right you can make it look like a lot. ☞

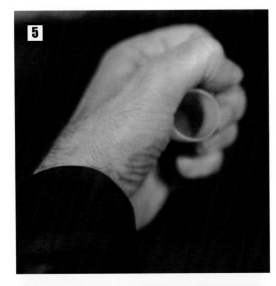

Don't fill the thumb tip – a quarter- or half-full is enough: you have to leave enough room to get your thumb inside or the trick won't work. Put the salt cellar back on the table. As you do this, the fingers of your left hand work the open top end of the thumb tip back until it's projecting from the rear of the fist **(5)**. The fist tilts slightly towards the spectators.

No one should see you make this adjustment because the larger movement of putting the salt cellar on the table covers the small movement of the left hand. "That might be a bit too much. Let me just get rid of those loose grains off the top." Your right hand now comes over the left as if to wipe off a few loose grains of salt. As it does, the right thumb is pushed into the thumb tip **(6)**. The thumb tip is stolen away as your right palm makes a couple of brushing gestures across the top of your left fist. Move your right hand away with the back towards the audience and the thumb tip nearest to you so that it's behind your fingers **(7)**.

Say, "Watch closely: we start with the salt in the left hand," and blow towards your left hand. Slowly open the left hand, finger by finger. "It's gone." Bring your palms together and brush both hands backwards and forwards a couple of times against each other as though the trick's over. The motion keeps the thumb tip invisible. Then drop both hands to your sides. "But it's not gone far. It's actually travelling up my left sleeve." Look towards your left sleeve as if following the salt as it makes its journey. Shrug your left shoulder as if trying to shift the salt over a bony hurdle. "Oops. Over the shoulder. That's it – and across the back." Turn your head to the right as you continue to follow the imaginary migration. "Down the right sleeve – tricky little turn at the elbow. Along the wrist and... here it is!"

While you've been tracking the salt, you've closed your right hand into a fist with the thumb tip inside it and removed your thumb so that it's in much the same position in which it started in the left hand. Now raise your right fist and tip it over ever so slowly, allowing the salt to pour out in a fine stream **(8)**. If you don't want to make a mess, catch it on a plate, an ashtray or in a cup.

When all the salt has poured out, reinsert your right thumb into the thumb tip and in a continuing motion brush your hands together, the same as before, in what appears to be a natural move to wipe your hands clean of the last grains.

It also allows the spectators to see your hands apparently empty without inviting any close scrutiny.

NOTES

In this routine, the salt disappears from one hand and appears in the other, but you can make the salt appear from somewhere else entirely. One good way is to borrow a banknote. Show it on both sides and then roll it up into a tube around the thumb which has the tip on it. Leave the thumb tip with the salt inside the tube as you take it in the other hand. Wave your free hand over the tube in a pseudo-mystical way and then tip the tube over to pour out the salt. Stick your thumb back into the rolled note and steal away the thumb tip as you unroll it and hand it back to the owner.

You can produce or vanish pretty much anything you can fit into the thumb tip. You can even use the gimmick to transform one object into another. For instance, to change salt into sugar you just need to have one or two sugar cubes palmed in your right hand. Perform the first part of the salt routine as written, secretly transferring the thumb tip into the left fist. Pour the salt into the fist and into the thumb tip.

However, as you steal the tip away on the right thumb you open the left fist a little and let the sugar cubes drop into it from the right hand. Tell the audience that you're going to transform the salt into sugar. "Now, you might be wondering how you'll be able to tell whether or not it's really changed; after all, they do look very similar. Well, it's easy: salt doesn't come in cubes!" You open your hands and tip the sugar cubes out on to the table.

A visit to your local magic shop or one of the many magic dealers on the Internet will reveal a whole variety of thumb tips for sale. These range from the cheapest, found in children's magic sets, to custom-moulded prosthetic pieces created by special effects technicians.

Whichever version you use, the real secret is to forget that you're wearing it. As mentioned earlier, it's not generally the colour of a thumb tip that will give it away; it's more likely to be your body language while using it. One of the magic's greatest sleight-of-hand experts was Dai Vernon. Magicians called him "The Professor" because of his dedication and mastery of the craft. His greatest piece of advice to magicians was "Be natural". It's advice well worth following, and can be applied to every single trick in this book.

ON THE NAIL

You're feeling lucky. You look at someone, write something on a pad of paper and then ask them to call out a number between one and ten. When you reveal your prediction, you're absolutely spot-on. You repeat the trick, this time asking two people to think of numbers. Again you write down your prediction. They call out their numbers and when they're totalled they add up to the very same number you wrote on the pad.

The secret gimmick used in this trick is called a "nail writer", sometimes known as a "swami gimmick". It comes in many different types, but basically they are all tiny bits of pen or pencil that can be attached to your thumb **(1)**.

You use this gimmick to secretly write on the pad after the spectators have revealed the numbers they thought of. Writing with the nail writer isn't easy. You need to hold the pad with both hands. The right thumb should be at right angles to the surface of the pad **(2)**.

Learn to write in firm, bold strokes. And, having done that, learn to duplicate that style of writing when you use a pencil. It's no use if the writing made with the nail writer doesn't match the writing you would normally make with a pencil, especially in the routine that follows. Here's the presentation.

You have a pad, a pencil and, assuming that you are right-handed, the nail writer on your right thumbnail. You don't have to worry about people catching a glimpse of the nail writer because

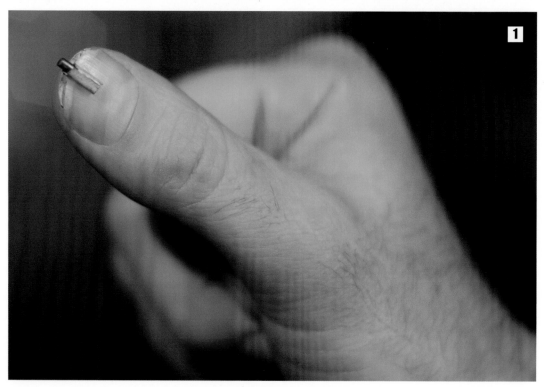

1

it's so easy to hide it behind the pad you're holding. Start with a couple of psychological stunts to get the spectators in the right frame of mind. Write down the number seven on the pad, hidden from the spectators' view, and then ask everyone to quickly think of a number between one and ten.

Everyone can participate in this. Turn your pad around to reveal the number seven and ask how many people thought of this number. Sometimes an amazingly high proportion of your spectators will tell you that they did actually think of seven. This is simply psychology: seven is a number many people gravitate towards when asked to choose a number between one and ten. Tell the spectators this fact and comment on how much their choice reflected the findings of psychologists.

Sometimes it works and sometimes it doesn't. Tear off the top sheet of the pad and offer to try another experiment. "This time, think of a two-digit number between one and 50. It must be an odd number and the two digits should be different, so 22 doesn't count!" As they do, you write the number 37 on your pad. "Okay: an odd number with two digits between one and 50. Did anyone get 37?" Turn the pad around to reveal the number. Again, a large percentage of your spectators will probably have thought of the same number. If you think about the options, the conditions you laid down really restrict which numbers they can choose and, of ☞

those, 37 is by far the most popular choice. "Again, this isn't mind-reading; it's psychology. If you analyze what I said, you'll see how I led you to the number 37. Let's try something else." Tear off the top sheet, and this time only pretend to write something down on your pad. Put the pencil aside or in your pocket. Select one of the spectators and ask them to listen very carefully. "I'm going to start calling out the numbers one to ten. At any time you feel like it, I want you to call "Stop". Stop me on any number you want, okay?"

Start calling out numbers. Make it interesting, calling them out fast and slow and with slightly different intonations as if working another psychological trick and trying somehow to trap the spectator into choosing a particular number. If you get to the number ten before "Stop" has been called, start calling them out again backwards. Sooner or later, however, the spectator should stop you on a number. Repeat that number and, as you do, hold the pad close to your chest and secretly write the chosen number on the top sheet with your nail writer while maintaining eye contact with the spectator. Asking him why he stopped on that particular number will help give you time to do your secret writing, as well as providing misdirection for the action.

Finally, turn the pad around to show that you wrote down exactly that number. Tear off the top sheet, pick up the pencil and tell the spectators that you'll try one final experiment. Pretend to write a two-digit number on the pad. Then place the pencil aside and hold the pad close to your chest. Select two spectators to help. Ask the first spectator to look at the second spectator: "Really study her.

Look at the way she looks, the way she dresses, the colour of her eyes. Now give me a two-digit number, quick as you can." They follow your rather bizarre instructions and call out a number. Let's say it's 27. Now ask the second spectator to return the favour. She's to look at the first spectator and call out a number. Let's say she chooses 44. As soon as you know both numbers you mentally total them ($27 + 44 = 71$) and you secretly write this number on the pad. Then ask each of the spectators what they saw in the other which made them call out their numbers.

Make the most of their responses. "Well, unfortunately I didn't get 27 or 44," you say. Turn the pad around to reveal the number 71. "But here's the weird thing; you see, I wasn't just looking at one of you. I was looking at both of you." Pick up the pen and write the numbers 27 and 44 above your 71. Then openly add the two chosen numbers to reveal the total. The spectators will be amazed to see that they add up to 71 – the same number you predicted. Ditch the nail writer in your pocket as you casually put the pencil away.

NOTES

It's difficult to write entire words with a nail writer but it's not difficult to write down individual letters of the alphabet. You can therefore predict, say, someone's initials.

You can also easily mark ticks and crosses, so you could, for instance, write down a list of five animals and then ask someone to think of one. You appear to put a tick against one of the items on the list. In reality, you do nothing at all, but you nail-write a tick or cross against the thought-of animal as soon as the spectator has revealed it. You can do the same with a chosen number on a lottery ticket.

An impressive trick is to produce your prediction of a chosen number out of a sealed envelope. The envelope appears to make the use of any secret writing techniques an impossibility. In fact, it makes the use of a nail writer even more deceptive. Prepare for the trick by taking a blank business card or postcard and on it, in

writing which matches your nail writer, write the phrase: "You will think of the number . . ." leaving the number part blank. The card is sealed in a small envelope, but unknown to the audience the envelope has a hole cut out of it and this hole lies immediately over the blank space.

To perform the trick, introduce the sealed envelope and place it on the table, hole side down. Ask someone to call out a number between one and ten. Pick the envelope up and open it. As you open it, use the nail writer to write the chosen number through the hole and on to the card **(3)**. Take the card out of the envelope and hand it to someone to read. While they read out the contents of the card, you ditch the envelope and nail writer in your pocket.

As I mentioned earlier, there are many different models of nail writer on the market. Some of them are modified thumb tips, others

write with ink rather than pencil – although I've never found a reliable one of those. The best advice I can give you on the nail writer is "Practice, practice, and more practice." You need to be able to write without ever looking at your hands – and never write when other people are looking directly at your hands. The best time is when everyone's attention is elsewhere, usually on another spectator who is carrying out some task.

As with all magic, the secret is to believe you really can do what you claim. Then your body language doesn't give away the sneaky and sometimes complicated things you have to do to make the trick effective. And make sure you know the routine so well that the mechanics of it are working on an almost subconscious level: many a good trick has been ruined by a performer who hasn't rehearsed enough. Don't let that be you.

ON THE PULL

You place a key in your hand, it vanishes. You show a coin and squeeze it until it's bent in half. You take a handful of change from your pocket and it disappears. These are just a few of the incredible effects made possible using a utility device that magicians call a "pull".

The most common type of pull works with a length of elastic. Thin black cord elastic is best. One end is tied to the object you want to make vanish – a key, for instance – and the other end is tied to a safety pin **(1)**. The pin is fastened inside your jacket at the top of the right sleeve so that the key hangs down inside your sleeve, just above the edge of the cuff **(2)**. In this position you can move the hand about freely and no one will spot the key.

When you want to perform the vanishing key trick, you casually bring the hands together and, with the left fingers, reach up the sleeve and pull the key down into the right hand. You don't want to be seen doing this preparation, so do it when the audience's attention is elsewhere. You can gain complete cover for the move by putting your hands behind your back while you do it. Either way, let's assume you now have the key secured in the closed fingers of the right hand.

Ask the audience if they've seen that guy on television who pretends that he can bend keys using the power of his mind. And then tell them that you have been practising. "It's not quite working out: let me show you what I mean." You reach into your pockets with both hands as if searching for a key. This is all bluff, because the key you're going to use is the one that's attached to the elastic pull.

Bring the right hand out of the pocket, holding the key at the fingertips **(3)**. The point at which the key is tied is hidden by the right thumb and fingers. The elastic runs along the near side of the wrist and isn't visible to the audience. Hold the key up so that everyone gets a good look at

it. Then breathe on it, explaining, "The first thing you have to do is warm the key up slightly, like this." This is just an excuse to give them a decent chance to see the key in your hand. Open the left hand and place the key into it. The left fingers close around the key **(4)**.

As they do, the right hand relaxes its grip on the key and allows the elastic to pull it quickly up the sleeve and out of sight. The right hand falls by the side as the closed left hand is held out for everyone to see. "Look – it's happening." Rub the fingers of the left fist together as if the key's becoming softer. Everyone will think that the key is somehow bending inside your hand. But you surprise them by slowly opening your fingers, one at a time, to reveal that the key has melted away completely. "It happens every time" you say, "I must be rubbing too hard!"

The Vanishing Key is just one of many tricks you can perform using a pull. Here are a few more variations.

Vanishing Coin

Instead of a key, drill a hole near the edge of a large coin. Attach one end of the elastic to the coin and the other end inside the sleeve as before. With this gimmick you can pretend to take out a coin from your pocket and make it disappear exactly as you did the key. It's a very clean vanish and only requires a bit of acting ability to make it into a truly puzzling piece of magic.

Bending Coin

If you add a little sleight-of-hand you can go even further. Get a coin which matches the coin you attached to the elastic. Cover it in a piece of cloth and then bend it in half using a pair of strong pliers and a vice. The cloth prevents the coin from being marked by the tools while you're bending it. Have this bent coin in the right-hand jacket pocket and the coin on the pull in the right sleeve. This ☞

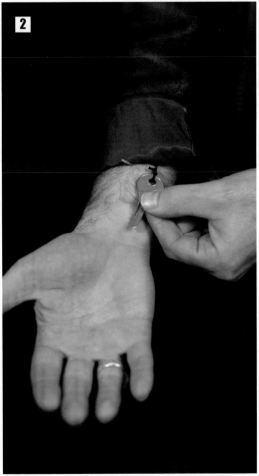

time, as you reach into the pocket to pull out a coin, you classic-palm the bent coin. Display the coin which is attached to the pull at the fingertips and tell the audience about your amazing metal-bending powers. Pretend to place the coin in the left hand but as you do, let the palmed coin fall into the left hand as the coin on the pull shoots up the right sleeve. Squeeze the coin in the left fist and ask someone to hold their hands out below, ready to catch the coin. "Be careful," you say, "it can get quite hot." Open the left fingers and allow the bent coin to fall into the spectator's waiting hands. They won't just be surprised that the coin is now bent but, if you "sell" the trick properly, many of them will be convinced that the coin is actually hot!

Disappearing Change

So far you've learned how to vanish or change a single object, but using the pull you can make several objects disappear at once: at least, you could if you could prevent the objects rattling together as they travelled up your sleeve. Here's one simple way to meet that challenge. Using some superglue, make a gimmick which consists of several coins stuck together in a fan. The coins shouldn't all be the same denomination: you want to make the fan of coins look as if you could have picked it up from a handful of loose change.

The fan of coins has a hole drilled through it at one end and is attached to the elastic as before **(5)**. This time, when you perform the trick you actually do take a handful of change from your left pocket. Then you reach in among the change with the right hand, apparently picking up several of the coins. In fact, you don't pick any of these coins up. Instead, you push the fan of coins which is already hidden in the fingers of the right hand into view.

Hold the gimmicked coins up as if you've just taken them from the left hand **(6)**. Drop the change back into the left pocket as you show the fan of coins. Pretend to place the coins in the left hand, but really allow them to shoot up the sleeve as usual. Close the left hand, wave the empty right hand over it and reveal that the coins have all disappeared. It seems absolutely impossible for a handful of coins to have completely evaporated under these conditions.

Make the most of it. There's one point to remember when making this gimmick. The elastic should be attached at the narrow end of the fan, not in the middle. This allows the gimmick to be drawn up the sleeve longways rather than sideways so that it doesn't catch on the edges of your sleeve.

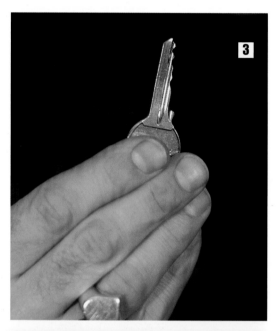

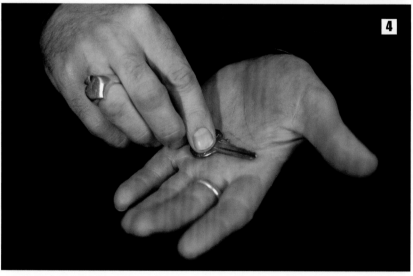

NOTES

There's really no end to the variety of vanishes and transformations you can perform with a pull. The secret, as with most magic, is to be able to use the pull in a natural manner. You shouldn't look as if you're struggling to hold on to something which is attached to you. You have to behave as naturally while working the pull as if it didn't exist. As usual, any unnatural body language will make the audience suspicious.

Try different kinds of elastic until you get one that stretches easily, and adjust the position of the pull in your sleeve so that you can always get access to the object. It should lie a couple of inches above the edge of the sleeve when the elastic is relaxed, and the elastic should be strong enough that you can be confident it will quickly draw the object out of sight when necessary.

Equally important is the get-ready; the moment the left fingers reach up into the right sleeve to retrieve the pull. Always do this when no one's paying attention to you. If sitting, you can do it when you hands are below the table. If standing, take an opportunity to step back briefly from the action or behind someone or, as mentioned earlier, simply put your hands behind your back. Try to make the preparation a reasonable length of time before you go into the trick.

One final tip: some magicians prefer to have a pull which is elastic for most of its length but is actually fine fishing line for the last six inches or so. They tie the length of elastic to the length of fishing line, and it's the fishing line which is attached to the coin or key. The reason for this is that the fishing line is virtually invisible and far less likely to be spotted by the audience than the much thicker black elastic. Try it: you might find it gives you far greater confidence and freedom when handling the gimmick.

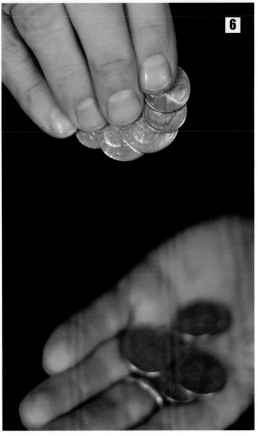

SMOKE AND MIRRORS

Cigarettes damage your health: everyone knows that. What isn't so well known is that cigarettes can damage almost everything else they come into contact with too. In this trick, you seem to push a cigarette right through a borrowed coin! (1).

Over the years, magicians have created all kinds of mechanical coins to aid them in their wizardry, and this trick uses one of the most ingenious. It's a coin which has a tiny round trapdoor at its centre. When the trapdoor is closed, even close-up, it's almost impossible to see: the coin has been made by a master mechanic.

But if you push a cigarette against it, the door will open and the

cigarette can be pushed right through **(2)**. The photo shows an exposed view from the side.

You can buy a coin like this from any magic store either in your high street or on the Internet – it's known, rather unimaginatively, as the Cigarette Through Coin trick! To perform the trick, you have to borrow a coin which matches yours from one of your spectators

1

and then switch it for the gimmicked coin. You push the cigarette through the gimmicked coin and then switch the coins again to finish.

It's not a particularly difficult trick to do. And because no one suspects that there are such things as trick coins, the effect on the spectators is way out of proportion to the simplicity of the method.

There are many ways of choreographing this routine and I'll mention some others in the notes later, but for now you might like to give this handling a try. Start with the gimmicked coin in the right pocket. Reach into your pockets as you say, "I just need a coin for this." Name the same denomination as your gimmicked one. Classic-palm the gimmicked coin in your right hand but

pretend that you can't find a coin of the right size, so turn to one of the spectators and ask them whether they've got one they could lend you. Take the coin from the spectator with your left hand. This allows everyone to see that hand empty without actually calling attention to it.

Now turn to someone who smokes and ask if you can borrow a cigarette. "Don't worry: you'll get it back." This activity takes the heat off the coin and you now have plenty of time to switch it.

Do this by casually passing the borrowed coin to the right hand and then drop the right hand by your side as you reach out with your left hand to take the cigarette **(3)**. You now switch the coin using a sleight known as the DeManche Change. ☞

First, let the palmed gimmicked coin drop on to the fingers **(4)**. Be careful that it doesn't clink against the borrowed coin. Then, with the second finger, push the coin along the underside of the thumb and into the classic palm **(5)**. This is almost the same technique you learned when studying the classic palm in the Midas Touch chapter. As soon as the switch is made, raise the right hand and push the gimmicked coin to the fingertips with the hole side facing the spectators and the trapdoor side towards you **(6)**. You now have a cigarette in the left hand, the coin in the right. Sniff the cigarette, saying, "Nasty! It's not just bad for your lungs; it's bad for everything else – watch."

Place the end of the cigarette against the surface of the coin and start to move it around as if looking for a weak spot. "It won't take a moment. You don't even need to light it." When you've positioned the cigarette directly over the trapdoor, slowly push it into the coin.

The cigarette need only be an eighth of an inch into the coin and you can let go with your left hand. At this point the cigarette just looks like it's clinging to the coin **(7)**. Spectators don't realize yet that it's started to penetrate through. "Weird, isn't it? It's stuck. That's the tar in the tobacco!" Bring the left hand back to the cigarette, push on the other end and force the cigarette through the trapdoor and through the coin. The coin is now halfway along the cigarette. It looks amazing. Move the right hand away again so that

dramatic movement and then hold the cigarette high as you say, "This is yours," before handing it back to the spectator who loaned it. You now use the sleeving technique from Devalued to switch the coin back. Let the gimmicked coin lie flat on the left palm. Then say, "Now we just have to heal the hole up," and as you apparently bring the right hand over to rub the coin, you shoot it up the right sleeve and drop the borrowed coin in its place. This leaves you clean, with just the borrowed coin in your hands which you hand back to the spectator, "And this is yours". Watch the scurry to examine it.

NOTES

Another way of switching the gimmick for the borrowed coin is by using the technique from Inflation. Encourage the spectator to take a look at his cigarette, and with the gimmicked coin held between the thumb and fingertips of the left hand, the right hand drops briefly to the side, releasing the palmed coin on to the right fingers. You bring the right hand back up and cover the gimmicked coin ("rubbing away the hole.") Let the gimmicked coin fall on to the base of the left fingers and replace it with the borrowed coin, hidden behind the right fingers.

Continue the action by rubbing the surface of the coin with the right fingertips, gradually revealing more and more of the coin to the spectators. The right hand then takes the coin and hands it back while the left hand drops to the side and classic-palms the gimmicked one. Game over.

The first part of the trick, switching in the gimmicked coin, is the easiest. Switching the coin out after a cigarette has apparently passed through it is much more difficult, which is why your palming skills have to be top-notch.

the spectators can appreciate the effect, but be careful that you don't let anyone see the trapdoor at the back of the coin. You do have to be extremely careful with your angles. If in doubt, lower the hand and hold the coin so that it faces upwards towards the ceiling or sky. That way, everyone will have to look down at it and the trapdoor will be harder to spot. "Okay," you say, "let's go all the way through." As you say this, the left fingers and thumb take hold of the coin. The right hand forefinger and thumb then take hold of the inner end of the cigarette and pull it right through the coin while still holding the borrowed coin hidden in the palm. Do this in one

Chapter four
HANDS ON DECK

Magicians love card tricks – they usually make up the vast majority of their repertoires. The deck of cards is the ultimate magical device – 52 identities, 13 values, four suits and two colours allow for inexhaustible magical possibilities. When learning card routines, go for variety – you don't want every trick to consist of someone choosing a card and you finding it. The tricks in this chapter are not difficult – learn three or four that gradually grow in impossibility. And don't over-use them. Remember: always leave them wanting more!

CARD CRIME

A spectator chooses a card from the deck, remembers it and replaces it. The deck is cut several times and the card lost. But not for long, because you can find the card using a little forensic magic. One look at the spectator's thumb leads you to the only playing card in the deck that he's touched – the card he selected just moments ago.

This trick uses what's known as a Key Card. It's a card you spotted earlier in the trick and secretly positioned next to the selected card to help you to find it. Here's how it works. Take the deck of cards and hold it in your right hand in preparation for an overhand shuffle. Peel cards off the top of the deck into the left hand, just a few at a time, and ask the spectator to call out 'stop' at any time **(1)**.

When he does, stop taking cards, separate the hands and thumb-off the top card of the left-hand packet. Ask him to take, look at and remember this card. As he does this, your right hand tilts towards you so that you can take a sneaky peek at the bottom card of the packet **(2)**. This will be your key card. When the spectator has remembered his card, ask him to put it back where he got it from; on top of the left-hand packet. Immediately drop the right-hand packet on top of the left-hand cards. This puts your key card immediately above the spectator's selected card. Square the deck and give it a simple cut, cutting off the top half of the deck and placing it underneath the bottom half. 'I'm going to give the deck two cuts and I want you to do the same.' Make another cut and then hand the deck to the spectator. Ask him to do exactly what you did; give the pack two complete cuts.

Watch him to make sure he doesn't do anything other than that because, curiously, the cuts won't do anything to upset your trick but a shuffle would. When the deck is handed back to you your key card will still be on top of the spectator's selected card. And because you've given the cards an even number of cuts, the chances are that they'll both be somewhere near the middle of the deck. Try it and see.

By this time the spectator should be convinced that you've no idea what or where his card is: you didn't see it, it went back into the middle of the deck and the deck's been cut several times. How could you possibly find the card? Easy – forensic science! "Card tricks are a puzzle. They're like those crime stories you see on TV; a murder mystery. And you, my friend, are the murderer.

"Question is – who's the victim? I'm going to take a scientific approach. Can I see your thumb, please – your right thumb?' This request might get a puzzled look, but you insist on seeing his thumb. Persuade him to stick it up in the air as if hitching a ride, then pull it towards you and take a good look. If you want to get a laugh at this point, take out a magnifying glass and examine his thumb as if you were Sherlock Holmes.

"What I'm looking at is your thumbprint: everyone's thumbprint is different. And I noticed that when you chose your card you gripped it with your right thumb pretty much dead-centre. You'll have left a big fat print there, my friend. Let me see if I can find it." Ask a different spectator to hold out their hand, palm upwards, to play the part of a makeshift table. Start dealing cards from the top of the deck face-up on to their hand **(3)**.

Tell the spectator who chose the card, "Now, I don't want you intimidating the witnesses by staring at them, so close your eyes for a moment." Continue dealing through the cards. Every now and then stop and pick up one of the cards from the face-up pile. Hold it alongside the spectator's thumb – the one who has his eyes closed – as if comparing the invisible print on the card with the print on his thumb. "Nope, that's not it: that's mine," you say, as you place the card back on the pile. "That's the girl I did the trick with last night..." Eventually you'll deal your key card on to the face-up pile. You now know that the next card dealt will be the spectator's. Stop as soon as you see it. "Get me a warrant. I think I've found it."

Take the card and hold it against the spectator's thumb for comparison. "Yep: that's the victim. Squeezed to death." Ask the spectator to name the card he chose and then open his eyes. He should be amazed to see that it's the one you're holding. ☞

2

3

NOTES

You don't have to spot your key card as the spectator takes his card. You can spot the bottom card of the deck before you even start the trick. That way no one will ever see you catch a glimpse of it. Often I'll make a mental note of the bottom card of the deck while the spectator is handling it during another trick. That way I can go straight into the trick and no one suspects a thing.

It doesn't matter how many times the deck is cut, the key card will always stay with the selection. The only exception is when the cards are cut so that the key card is the face/bottom card of the deck and therefore the last card you deal. If that happens, the chosen card will be the first card you dealt. That's no problem; just finish by pulling out the first card again from the bottom of the pile: the spectator who chose it has no idea where you plucked the card from – he still has his eyes shut! ✋

JACK SANDWICH

A card is selected, remembered and returned to the deck. You riffle the end of the deck with a snap and two cards magically turn face-up – the two black Jacks. Unfortunately neither of them is the selected card. The Jacks are replaced in the deck but left face-up and the deck is cut several times. Finally the cards are spread out to reveal that the two black Jacks have now trapped one card between them. It is, of course, the chosen card.

This uses the key card handling in a slightly different way. Before you perform the trick, you must take out the two black Jacks and place them face-up at the bottom of the face-down deck. When you bring out the deck, don't reveal the presence of the face-up Jacks. Begin by holding the deck face-down in the right hand and shuffle off some cards into the left hand as you ask a spectator to call out "Stop" any time they like; the same selection procedure as used in the Card Crime trick. Thumb off the top card of the left-hand packet and ask the spectator to look at and remember it before putting it back.

Drop the right-hand packet of cards on top of the selection and square the deck. You can, if you wish, now shuffle off a few more cards from the top to the bottom of the deck. Just be careful not to disturb the cards in the middle of the deck, which is where your two face-up Jacks now lie. Tell the spectator that you'll snap your fingers and make the selected card turn face-up in the deck. Snap your fingers, but do it twice. Spread the deck between your hands to reveal that there are now two cards face-up in the middle of the deck – the two black Jacks **(1)**. "Oops: sorry. Should have only ☞

done that once – is either of those the card you chose?" They aren't, so you offer to use the black Jacks to find their selection.

Take all the cards which lie above the face-up jacks and put them to the bottom of the deck. Then spread the top few cards so that the Jacks can be seen **(2)**. "The black Jacks will find your card: let me show you." Because of your handling earlier, the card immediately below the Jacks is the spectator's selection. Square up the cards in the left hand but, as you do, stick your left little finger under the third card from the top so that it keeps a break between the top three cards and the rest of the deck **(3)**.

The photo shows an exposed view from the side. From the spectator's point of view, the break is totally invisible. With your right hand, lift off the top three cards

together. The right fingers are at the front of the packet and the thumb at the inner end **(4)**. The left thumb then peels the top card of this packet back on to the deck and pushes it forward slightly so that it overhangs at the front. This is known as an "outjog" **(5)**. From the

audience's point of view you are just displaying the two face-up black Jacks, but in reality you have the spectator's selection hidden under the right-hand Jack. Place this Jack under the deck so that it sticks out a little at the inner end. This is known as an "injog" **(6)**. Be careful that you don't expose the face-down card hidden below it.

"Two Jacks with another fifty cards between them and one of them's yours. Watch the Jacks go into action." Square the Jacks up so that they're flush with the deck and then give the deck a complete cut. Hand it to the spectator, inviting him to give the deck a second cut. Make sure he completes the cut, taking a block of cards from the top and placing them on the bottom. Then ask him to give the deck one more cut, "for luck". That's three cuts in total. To the audience, it's the equivalent of mixing up the cards but, as explained in the previous trick, this cutting procedure doesn't alter the sequence of cards. What the cuts have done is brought the two black Jacks together either side of the selected card. Snap your fingers over the deck and then ask the spectator to spread the cards slowly between his hands. He'll find your two black Jacks face-up in the centre, but now there's a single face-down card between them **(7)**.

Reach into the spread and take out this three-card sandwich. Ask him to name his chosen card, then turn the three cards over to reveal that they've succeeded in finding his selection.

NOTES

If the spectator looks a bit clumsy with his handling of the cards, then take the deck back from him and spread it out yourself. Do it slowly and openly – you don't want anyone thinking that you're doing anything sneaky at this stage. If you master the ribbon spread, described in the Cruising chapter later, you can use that to make a flashier finish.

CARD COUNTER

This is something your audience will always remember: a strange magical novelty in which you turn a spectator's credit card into a pretend Geiger counter. The credit card makes a clicking sound as it's dragged along the spread of cards on the table. As the clicking reaches its loudest point, you detect the chosen card!

As well as a spectator who's willing to lend someone as untrustworthy as you their credit card, you'll also need a marker pen with ink which will dry quickly when applied to a playing card. And for the yarn you're about to spin, the more unusual the pen looks, the better. Begin the trick by handing the pen out for examination, telling the spectator that it uses an ink which contains a specially formulated chemical. "Look – I'll prove it."

Ask if anyone has a credit card on them and then have that person select a card from the deck you're holding, but tell them not to look at it. They're just to pull it from the deck and place it face-down on the table. "Great: now write your name on the back of the card." Hand them the pen. As they're writing on the back of their chosen card you casually glance down at the deck in your hand and get a sneaky glimpse of the bottom card. This will be your key card. Put the deck on the table as soon as you've got the information. When the spectator has finished writing, take the pen back and put it away. "Now cut the deck in two." Point to what was the top half of the deck and ask them to place their chosen card on it, and then to pick up the other half of the deck and place it on top of that. "Good. Now square the deck up and give it another cut. And another."

The spectator gives the deck two complete cuts. As mentioned previously, this cutting will not affect the position of your key card in relation to their card. They'll always be together apart from the one-in-52 chance that they'll be the top and bottom cards of the deck. "Be honest: do you have any idea where your card is?" He won't. "In fact, you not only don't know where the card is; you don't even know what it is, right?"

This is true. "That's where the special ink comes in." Pick up the deck and spread it across the table so that the index of all the cards can be seen (again, see the ribbon spread in the Cruising chapter). Ask the spectator to loan you a credit card. "This is going to sound a little odd. I told you that the ink in that pen was special. It is: in fact, it's… radioactive. And your credit card is a Geiger counter… don't look at me like that! I know it sounds a bit unlikely, but watch…" Take the spectator's credit card and slide its corner along the spread, from the face card to the top card **(1)**.

Hold the card very lightly, pressing its corner on to the spread of cards. A faint clicking sound will be heard as the credit card trips off the edges of the playing cards. As you run the credit card along, look out for your key card. The card directly next (underneath it in the face-up spread) will be the selection.

"I need to fine-tune this a bit…" Take the credit card and rub it on your sleeve as if trying to generate some static electricity or something. Then drag it along the spread of cards again, this time pressing down harder as the credit card nears the selection. As a result, the clicks get louder the nearer you get to the chosen card. Gently release the pressure on the credit card as you pass their card. The clicks get softer again. Run the credit card along the spread a third time, this time creating the loudest clicks you can manage as you approach the selected card. "Got it!" Stop on their card and use the credit card to push it forward out of the spread. "There's only one way to know whether this is your card or not. Turn it over." The spectator turns over the card and finds his signature on the other side. Give him back his credit card, saying, "I'd let that cool down for a while now if I were you!"

NOTES

The signature does mean that a card gets ruined every time you perform this trick, but I think it's worth it, and you can still use a deck that has half a dozen or more cards missing for many tricks without anyone noticing any difference in its thickness. The pen must, however, have quick-drying ink, otherwise it'll smudge and possibly mess up other cards. If no one trusts you enough to lend you their credit card (and if they had any sense, why would they?!), you can use your own or another distinctive playing card from the deck, for example a joker or the ace of Spades.

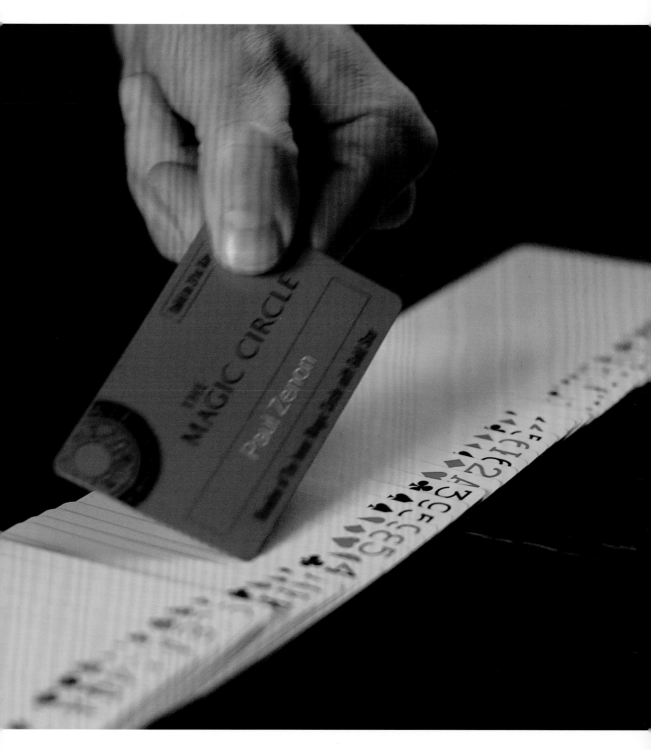

MAGIC SPELL

You tell the spectator exactly what you're going to do to find his chosen card. "Forewarned is forearmed", you might think: yet despite this and the impossible conditions under which the card is chosen, you make good on your promise, spelling out the phrase "This is your chosen card" to arrive at his selection. Best of all, the secret is so clever it might even fool you the first time you try it.

This trick introduces a new type of key card which you'll find useful in your magic. Instead of noting the face of the card, you put a slight bend in one of its corners called a "crimp" **(1)**. This means that you can locate it and cut to it again easily. An easy way to crimp the bottom card of the deck is to hold it in dealing position in your left hand and pull down on the inner right corner with your little finger **(2)**.

If you're sitting at a table opposite your spectator, the crimp will only be visible to you, and you can put it in easily and secretly while holding the deck and introducing the trick. "You might not know it, but there's a code among magicians – a set of rules that we stick to. For instance, we never reveal a secret. Well, not unless the money's right. And we never do card tricks on a Tuesday. Today's Tuesday? Well, I never was very good at sticking to the rules. But

the most important rule of all is that we never reveal in advance what we're about to do. It just spoils the surprise and gives you a chance to catch me out, right? Well, I'm going to take a walk on the wild side and break that rule too. I'm going to tell you exactly how this trick will end before it's even started."

By now you'll have crimped the corner of the bottom card of the deck and can start the trick proper. "Here's what I'm going to do: I'm going to ask you to take a card, remember it and put it back in the deck, and then I'm going to use a magic spell to find it. In fact I'm going to spell the phrase, 'This is your chosen card', and I'll deal one card for each letter, like this..." You demonstrate by dealing cards from the deck on to the table, one card for each letter in the phrase "This is your chosen card". That's 20 cards in all.

Pick up the next card from the deck and turn it face-up as you say, "And the very next card will be yours. Be amazing, wouldn't it? Well, I'd be amazed!" Put the card you've just shown back on top of the deck and then drop the deck on top of the pile of cards on the table. This positions your crimped card 21 cards up from the bottom of the deck. Square up the deck and leave it on the table.

"Let's start by choosing a card." Tell the spectator that you want him to divide the deck into three piles. Ask him to cut a really large packet of cards from the deck so that he just leaves a few cards on the table. This large packet is placed to the right of the smaller packet. Now ask him to cut off a few cards from the large packet

and place it to the right of that. This results in three packets of cards on the table with the largest in the middle, the former lower packet to its left and the former top packet to its right **(3)**. The photo shows the spectator cutting off the last packet. You can see the crimped card in the middle packet.

"Now you've cut some cards from the bottom and you've cut some cards from the top: no one could know the name of the new top card." You point to the top card of the middle packet. It's absolutely true; no one could know the name of this card. Ask the spectator to take a look at it, remember it and then put it back. "Let's lose your card so no one could possibly know where it ☞

is." Ask him to cut the large packet and complete the cut. He can give the packet several complete cuts until he's convinced that no one could know whereabouts his card lies. Take the packet from him, saying, "Of course, if I was a regular magician I'd be able to cut to your card like this." What you do is cut to the crimped card, taking it to the bottom of the packet. This is easy, because the bent corner creates a break at the inner end of the packet. Hold the packet in your left hand when making the cut. The right hand comes over the cards, the fingers at the outer end of the packet and the thumb lifting up at the break at the inner end directly under the crimped card.

With practice you can make the cut without looking and send the crimped card to the bottom of the packet. "But that's not what I said I'd do: I said I'd spell to your card." Drop the large packet on to the small packet which originally came from the top of the deck – the one on the right. And then pick up the small packet from the left which originally came from the bottom of the deck and drop it on top of everything. The spectator won't notice that you didn't reassemble the deck in its original order. Bizarrely, everything is now set for you

to spell out "This is your chosen card" and then turn up the next card to reveal the spectator's selection **(4)**. It's true: because of the mathematics of the cutting and your crimp, the chosen card is now 21st from the top of the deck. Try it and see! You can add a line here that makes the trick even more convincing. "I said I'd spell 'This is your chosen card' and the next card would be yours. But it'd be even better if you did the spelling – here, take the deck." Hand the deck to the spectator and let him spell to his own card.

NOTES

Sometimes you get lucky when the spectator is cutting the large middle packet to lose his card; he might cut directly to the crimped card for you, saving you the task. From here on, it looks like a miracle where the trick has performed itself.

You can actually use any phrase you like in the spelling. It makes it more personal if you include the spectator's name: for example, "This is John's chosen card" – ignore the apostrophe! The number of cards you spell out isn't critical but around 20 is best.

BIG DEAL

You reveal the secrets of the card sharps, showing everyone how to deal themselves four Kings in a game of poker. But a little knowledge can be a dangerous thing: just when the spectators think that they understand how the trick is done, you pull a last-minute switcheroo and deal yourself not four Kings but an even better hand – four aces.

This trick requires a set-up before you begin. Take out the four aces and place them on top of the deck. When you're ready, tell the spectators you'd like to give them a little lesson in cheating at cards. "The real secret is preparation, because what you don't know is that the card cheat secretly takes out four Kings and puts them on the bottom of the deck before he starts." **(1)** As you talk, openly take out the four Kings and place them on the bottom of the deck. Be careful not to flash the four aces on top. Let everyone see the four Kings clearly on the bottom of the deck **(2)**.

Then turn the deck face-down and hold it in the left hand ready to deal a game of poker. "The next move they use is something called the "bottom deal". Let's imagine this is a poker game with five players. The hustler deals the first round of cards like this." ☞

and it's much easier to get away with than you'd imagine. You're all staring at my hands at the moment, so the move's easy to see: but imagine this was a real game of cards. You wouldn't even be looking at me: you'd be looking at the cards I've dealt you."

For the fifth round of cards, you deal all the cards from the top of the deck. "The last card in my hand genuinely comes from the top. In fact, I'd subtly draw attention to that. I'd give a funny little little cough just before I dealt it; you'd all glance up and you'd see that my last card came from the top. And if the last card came from the top, then why wouldn't you assume that all the others had? See? It's all psychology."

Turn your hand of cards over to reveal that you've got four Kings and one indifferent card

Poker is a game with five cards in each hand and the dealer deals to himself last. So you deal out four cards, from left to right, to four imaginary players, and as you come to deal your card, you pause and say, "But when the cheat – that's me – deals to himself, he doesn't actually take the top card. He secretly deals a card from the bottom instead: let me show you." You openly reach under the deck with your left hand, take the bottom card and deal it on to the table as your card **(3)**. "Obviously I'm doing it slowly here so that you can see it." Continue to deal a second, third and fourth round of cards but each time you deal a card to your hand, you take the bottom card of the deck. "The bottom deal is a powerful weapon

(4). Don't change the position of any of the cards. "Four Kings – practically unbeatable. Now let me show you again at speed: try to spot the bottom deal if you can." Pick up your hand of cards and place the odd card on the face. Turn the hand face-down and drop it on top of the deck then gather up the other hands of cards.

You can gather the hands up in any order, but be careful you don't mix up the cards within each hand or the next phase of the trick won't work. As you're doing this, secretly crimp the bottom card of the deck and drop the collected hands of cards on top of the deck and give it a cut. This buries the hands in the middle of the deck, directly below the crimp. Invite one of the spectators to

give the deck another complete cut. You pick up the deck and give it a final cut, cutting the crimp back to the bottom. All this does is make it look like the deck is being mixed up. Actually, at the finish it will be in exactly the same order as when you began. "Did you spot what I was doing? That was called the 'gambler's cut'. It sets the Kings in position for the deal – watch."

Deal out five hands of poker, the last card in each round going to yourself. As you deal your card, do it with a bit of a snap, pulling it super-quick off the top of the deck. It looks a bit suspicious, which is exactly what you want: you want to convince the spectators that you're doing a bottom deal. "Did you see that? I'll try to get it down smoother on the next round." And sure enough, each time you deal the card for your hand, it looks less and less suspicious – not exactly difficult to achieve, since you are actually dealing all the cards from the top!

When you've dealt five cards for each hand, put the remainder of the deck aside. "Did any of you spot the move?" One or two spectators might say they did – suckers! "Okay, let's see what everyone else got." Start to turn over the other hands of cards. You'll find a King in the first hand. "Uh-oh. Damn – must have missed one. Doesn't matter, though: three Kings is still a good winning hand." Then you turn over a second hand. It too has a King – and so do the third and fourth hands. It looks like your demonstration of bottom dealing has gone horribly wrong; you missed every single King.

Let the spectators bask in your apparent failure. And then hit them with the capper. "Looks like I messed up... but then, that's just what a grifter would want you to think, because while you were busy looking for the Kings, I was busy finding the aces." Turn over your hand and reveal the four aces **(5)**. Boy, you're good!

NOTES

This is a classic poker cheating routine. I love the fact that you're leading the spectators up the garden path in order to hit them with an even better kicker at the end. You don't have to reveal the Kings in the other hands if you don't want to. If I want to perform the trick more quickly, I don't bother showing the four other hands: I just go straight for the finale and show the four aces in my hand. Then accept the applause as graciously as I can!

ACES HIGH

One of your spectators is also a card sharp but she doesn't know it yet. You ask her to cut the deck into four packets. She does. She then mixes the cards around a little and you ask her to turn over the top card of each packet. She does, and finds that somehow she's managed to find the four aces. How did she do it? She's no idea!

This trick is one of the easiest in the book and yet it's also one of the most impressive. Unknown to the spectator, you've already placed the four aces on top of the deck. Place the deck on the table in front of her and tell her, "I think you'd make a really good card sharp: let me look at your hands." Take a good look at them and tell her how sensitive they look. "No, I'm serious! You've definitely got the makings of a card sharp. Look; I'll show you what I mean."

Ask her to cut about a quarter of the cards from the top of the deck. She does. Then tell her to place this packet about a foot to the right of the rest of the deck **(1)**. "Good. Let's do it again. This time, cut about a third of the cards off." She cuts some more cards and you ask her to place them directly to the left of the previously cut packet. "Nice one; you are doing well." Bend down towards the table and squint at the cards as if gauging the number in each packet and trying to work out how many she should cut next. "This time, without thinking, just cut half the cards from the rest of the deck when I say "Three". Okay – one, two, three!" She makes the cut and places the packet to the left of the previous two packets.

This gives you four packets in a row. The four aces are now on top of the right-hand packet. "You ever done this before? No? You surprise me. Let's just even out the packets a little." Tell her to take the packet on the left and deal three cards from it on to the table at

the spot from which she's just picked it up, then deal one card on to each of the other three packets **(2)**. She then drops the packet back in its original position, but on top of the three cards she's dealt on to the table. "I love the way you deal. Class. You sure you never worked in a casino or anything?" Keep piling on the flattery and then ask her to pick up the next packet. Again she deals three cards

down on to the table, into the same position the packet occupied, and then one card on to each of the other three packets.

She finishes by dropping the packet she is holding on to the three cards she dealt on to the table. "Great. Couldn't have done better myself. You really are good!" Ask her to pick up the third packet and repeat the procedure, the packet being dropped on top of the three dealt cards once again. Finally she picks up the right-hand packet. This is the packet which originally had the four aces on top. Because of the dealing, it now has three random cards on top of those aces. "Almost there: deal three cards on to the table and then deal one card on to...oh, you know the score by now."

She does the same again, and then drops the packet on top of the three cards she dealt on to the table. "Now, have you got any idea why you've been doing what you've been doing for the past minute?" She hasn't, so you explain: "You are a natural-born card sharp. You cut the cards, and you mixed them up. But you also worked a bit of sleight-of-hand. How else can you explain this?" Slowly turn over the top card of each packet. Each one will be an ace **(3)**.

NOTES

You can make this trick even more impressive by looking as though you give the deck a shuffle before you start. Start with the four aces on top. Secretly crimp the bottom card of the deck. Now pick up the cards in overhand shuffle position. Drop the top half of the deck or so into the left hand. The aces are now on top of this left-hand packet.

Drop the right-hand packet on top of the left-hand packet. This puts the crimp above the aces. Take the deck in the right hand again and shuffle a few cards off into the left hand. You can shuffle off as many cards as you like so long as you stop before you reach the middle of the deck: this is where the aces are located.

Now drop the rest of the right-hand cards on top of the left-hand cards. With the cards in the left hand, make a cut at the crimp so that the crimp is the bottom card of the upper packet. Complete the cut so that the crimp becomes the bottom card of the deck. This positions the four aces back on top ready for the trick. You can repeat this shuffle-and-cut sequence several times as you're talking. Done casually, it subtly suggests that the deck can't be set up – and so you're ready to blow them away. 🖐

3

DEAD MAN'S HAND

You show a royal flush in spades and invite someone to choose one of the five cards. He remembers it and the hand of cards is shuffled back into the deck. Then you reveal that it was no ordinary hand of cards: it was the hand that Wild Bill Hickok was apparently dealt just before he was shot dead at the card table. It's been known as the "Dead Man's Hand" ever since.

You offer to invoke the spirit of Wild Bill in order to find the selected card. You spell out the words "Wild Bill" and "Dead Man's Hand", dealing a card for each letter. The very next card in the deck turns out to be the card that the spectator chose: a very strange coincidence.

But that's not all. A spectator deals five hands of poker as you tell everyone that when the spirit of Wild Bill is invoked, the Dead Man's Hand has a habit of falling to the person whose back is towards the door. Everyone takes a look at the cards they've been dealt. Suddenly there's a loud bang!

When everyone's calmed down they see that the man nearest the door has indeed been dealt a royal flush... in spades. This is a really fun routine to perform. In addition to a deck of cards, you need a small cap gun to produce the bang – the louder, the better. The gun is hidden in your pocket at the start of the routine. It's not a trick to do in airports or banks. Begin by offering to tell a strange story."It's the story of Wild Bill Hickok. Wild Bill was a gambler. In fact, he actually died at the card table, and the hand of cards he held at that time has been known ever since as the Dead Man's Hand. And this was it..."

Spread the deck with the faces towards you as you look for the royal flush in spades: the ten, Jack, Queen, King and ace. Separate these five

cards from the rest of the deck by pulling them out slightly from the rest of the deck wherever you locate them: this is known as an "upjog". As you look for these cards, you are also counting down 16 cards from the face of the deck, secretly putting a crimp in the lower left corner of the seventeenth card with your thumb **(1)**.

Don't include any of the royal flush cards in your count if they fall within this block of 17. Don't panic: this isn't as difficult as it sounds, but if you're worried you can do it secretly before you even start the trick. Close up the deck, pull out the royal flush and drop them face-up on to the table. "The royal flush in spades: many people consider it the most prestigious hand in poker. But it was also the hand that killed Wild Bill. Give them a shuffle." Hand the royal flush to one of the spectators and ask him to mix the cards, face-down. When he's finished, you ask him to square up the packet and take a secret peek at the bottom card. "Remember that card: it'll be important later." Let's assume he saw the ☞

ace of spades. With the right hand, cut the deck at the crimp you made and drop the upper half on to the table. Tell the spectator to drop his cards on top of it. You then drop the remainder of the deck on top of the others. Square the deck and ask the spectator to give it a complete cut. You then pick up the deck and give it a few more cuts, finishing by cutting your crimp to the bottom.

The position now is that the royal flush is below the 16 cards you secretly counted to earlier. "Gamblers are generally superstitious people: Wild Bill was no exception. They tend to trust little rituals to bring them luck. Here's one..." You start to deal out four hands of cards, from left to right across the table. You call out a letter for each card dealt, "W-I-L-D - that's the first word." Deal out a second round of cards on top of the first, again calling out a letter for each card dealt. "B-I-L-L - that's the second." Deal three more rounds of cards until you've got four hands of five cards on the table. As you deal each card you spell a letter, "D-E-A-D M-A-N-S H-A-N-D." Look at the spectator who chose the card and ask him to name it. Turn over the top card of the deck. It'll be his selection, the ace of spades **(2)**.

"It looks like Wild Bill is with us. Let's see if we can take it a little bit further..." Turn the chosen card face-down on top of the deck. Then gather up the four dealt hands of cards and drop them on top of the deck. As with Big Deal earlier, it doesn't matter in which order you gather the hands so long as you don't disturb the order of the cards in any individual hand. Amazingly, the deck is now set up for you to deal out five poker hands with the first hand dealt consisting of a royal flush in spades. "Let's play five hands of poker," you say.

"Why don't you deal?" Before handing the deck over, you've mentally selected one of the spectators. It will be the spectator who's sitting with his back directly to the nearest door. Since the first hand dealt will contain the royal flush, you hand the deck to the person to their immediate right. Then nominate five people who should be dealt cards. Naturally, this includes the man who's going to deal. He deals the first card to the man to his left and continues dealing left to right, dealing the fifth card to himself.

Let him carry on dealing five poker hands this way. While everyone's distracted with the dealing, you sneak the gun out of your pocket and hide it under the table, resting it on your leg. "In a moment I want you to look at your hands, but first let me tell you this: the legend of the Dead Man's Hand says that the royal flush in spades will always fall to the man with his back to the door.

Let's see if it's true." As soon as the spectators pick up their hands of cards, you fire the gun under the table. If you've built up the atmosphere sufficiently, the bang should make them jump out of their seats. As they recover, they'll see that the guy with his back to the door had indeed been dealt the Dead Man's Hand.

NOTES

This brilliant plot was originated many years ago by the magician Henry Christ. He used a hand of cards consisting of eights and aces which, according to legend, was the actual hand held by Wild Bill at the time of his death. Personally I think that a royal flush in spades is more obvious and memorable, especially as most people know that the ace of spades is popularly known as the Death Card. 🖐

PICKPOCKET

A deck of cards is wrapped up in a paper napkin and bound with a rubber band: then the spectator drops it into his jacket pocket. This unusual preparation is all part of a pickpocketing demonstration – allegedly. Reaching inside the spectator's pocket, you managed to instantly locate and remove his chosen card. What's more, the rest of the deck is still securely wrapped up. How did you manage to get that card out?

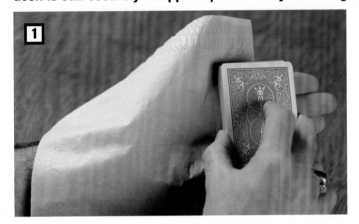

out the napkin and rubber band. "As I was saying, it was a device that Fagin used to test his accomplices' pickpocketing skills – using a genuine Dickensian rubber band and paper napkin!" While the spectators are looking at the props, you pick up the deck and give it a few cuts, casually taking the crimped card to the bottom while bringing the selection to the top. Take the deck in your right hand as you hold your left hand palm-up. Take back the napkin and place it over your hand so that the majority of it is over your wrist. You then place the deck on top of your napkin-covered palm **(1)**.

Adjust it to the position shown in the photo; you'll see how the majority of the napkin is to the left side of the deck. With your right hand, take the left side of the napkin and fold it over the deck **(2)**. ☞

This baffler once again uses the crimp to locate the spectator's card and then position it on top of the deck so that you can steal it away. In addition to the deck of cards, you need a paper napkin (or sheet of paper) and a rubber band that will stretch around the length of the deck. "This isn't really a trick," you explain. "It's an exercise that pickpockets use to practice. Charles Dickens mentioned it in Oliver Twist. Remember the bit where Fagin's testing out Oliver?" Dickens didn't actually mention this trick at all, but it's fun watching people nod their head in order to appear more well-read than they actually are!

Spread the deck face-down between your hands and ask someone to take a card. Square the cards in the left hand and, while the spectator's looking at his selection, crimp the bottom card of the deck. Take the deck in the right hand in overhand shuffle position and start to peel cards off into the left hand, asking the spectator to call "Stop" at any point. He places his chosen card on top of the left-hand packet and then you drop the rest of the cards on top.

This places your crimped card right above his selection. The beauty of the crimp is that you can now put the deck aside for a moment while you introduce the other items used in this trick. Hand

Do this as you explain that you're going to wrap the deck up securely. As you're talking, reach under the napkin with your right first and second fingers and secretly pull the top card, the selection, to the right so that it lies under the right side of the napkin **(3)**.

The photo shows an exposed view from below. In the same motion, fold the napkin around and under the deck, taking the card with it **(4)**. The selected card therefore ends up under the deck. Turn the entire wrapped deck over, end for end **(5)**. The chosen card remains hidden behind the napkin even though it's now separated from the rest of the deck: notice how the left side of the napkin is open. If you pulled open the napkin at this point, as in the photo, you'd actually see the selected card **(6)**. And in fact, if you wanted to, you could slide the selected card right out of the package at that point: but you don't. Instead, you secure the deck even more.

Fold the top and bottom parts of the napkin in on to the deck to form a neat package, and then take the rubber band and snap it around the deck lengthwise **(7)**. It appears as if you've securely wrapped and banded the deck, but in reality you can easily remove the selected card from the package without damaging the wrapping. Ask for a volunteer who's wearing a jacket, or someone who's carrying a bag. Drop the package inside their pocket or bag so that the open side is uppermost; we'll assume it's a pocket in

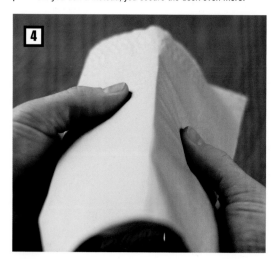

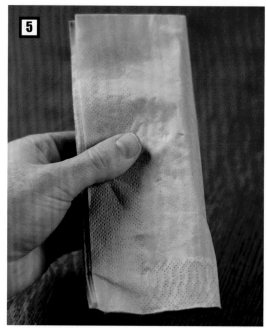

6

7

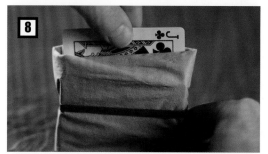

8

9

NOTES

The size of the napkin isn't crucial. It just needs to go around the deck at least once and you need to leave one side of the package open with the card under it. Once you know the size of napkin required to go around your deck, you can always adjust the starting position; if the napkin or paper is too big, just fold it in two or tear it in half before you start.

If you ever work this in a burger bar, borrow one of their take-out bags. Place the wrapped deck inside the bag but, as you do, secretly steal out the card and hold it inside the top of the bag. Hold the bag at the top, your fingers on the outside and your thumb on the inside, clipping the card in position. Then reach into the bag with your other hand and instantly produce the card in the same way as before.

This is a reputation-making trick: as you say goodbye to your friends, glance back and you can bet that they'll be checking their pockets to make sure all their belongings are still there!

this instance. You're almost set for the big finish. "In the old days, pickpockets had lots of ways of practicing. They'd hang up a jacket that had lots of tiny bells sewn to it and the thief had to reach into a pocket and steal whatever was there without making a sound.

But the test with the wrapped deck of cards was even harder: I'll show you why." Turn to the guy who chose the card and ask him what it was. Repeat the name of it and then stretch out your right hand, showing it empty. In slow motion, dip your hand inside the pocket as though you're having a practice run. While it's in there, reach into the open side of the package and secretly slide the card out until it's almost free of the napkin **(8)**. The photo shows an exposed view with the card half-way out.

Don't pull it all the way out of the pocket just yet; remove your empty hand from the pocket again. Cover this move by saying, "Okay, here's the deal: I'm going to dive into your pocket like this and I've got three seconds to find and remove your card. Just three seconds and it'll be done: watch me." Pause for effect with your hand hovering outside his pocket: "One, two... three!" Dip your hand in again and immediately pull out the selected card **(9)**.

"That was it, right? But that's not all: the difficult bit is to leave the parcel completely intact. Take it out: have a look." They do. They'll find the rest of the deck still wrapped and banded, with no clue as to how you could have stolen their card out so deftly.

GHOST CARD

Holding the deck upright in your hand, you throw a cloth napkin, handkerchief or headscarf over it. The cloth begins to move upwards as a card rises from the deck. The card, still covered, floats about a foot into the air until it's caught by the performer. The cloth is whipped away to reveal that the card is – you'd better believe it – none other than one selected by the spectator.

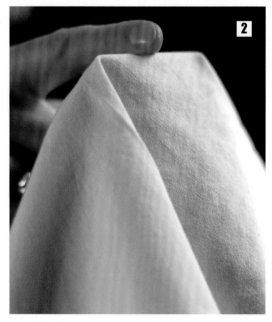

This trick is unbelievably simple but it looks really spooky. Have a card chosen, remembered and replaced. Control it to the top of the deck: I do this using the crimp card method described earlier. Hold the deck in the left hand with the faces towards the spectators. Tell them that you'll use static electricity to accomplish this particular trick, so you'll need to insulate the deck. Funny how often that old static comes in handy for tricks, isn't it? Borrow a cloth napkin or headscarf and drape it over the deck **(1)**.

Close your right hand into a fist and then extend your forefinger. Rub the forefinger backwards and forwards across your left sleeve as if trying to generate some static – all just showmanship again: nothing to do with the actual method. Touch your forefinger to the top of the covered deck and then instantly pull your hand away as if you just felt an electric shock. Pause, rub the finger on your sleeve again and then touch it to the top of the covered deck once more (masochist that you are!) This time, with your left thumb you push upwards on the top card of the deck. This is the one that was chosen. Keep pushing until the card pushes the fabric upwards.

The spectators see something rising under the cloth. At the same time, raise your right hand so that it looks as if your finger is attracting the card and cloth and pulling them up with it **(2)**.

Push the top card as far as it will go with your thumb and then extend your right little finger and hook it under the bottom edge of the card through the cloth **(3)**. The photo shows an exposed view,

3

but so long as the spectators are standing in front of you they won't see this fiddle. You'll find that the right hand now has total control of the selected card. It's gripped between the forefinger at the top and the little finger at the bottom. Continue to raise the right hand high above the deck. From the front, it appears as if a card is floating in the air under the cloth: it looks really weird! **(4)**

Ask the spectator to name the card he chose. When it's about a foot or 18 inches above the deck, catch the top of the card between the right thumb and forefinger and curl in your other fingers. Flip it upside-down so that the napkin falls over your hand to reveal the chosen card staring everyone in the face **(5)**.

NOTES

This is a really cool trick; simple, yet it has a great effect on the audience. Obviously you can't have anyone standing next to you while you work it, otherwise they'll see how it's done, but other than that it's highly practical. The better your acting, the better this trick will be. Try to make it look as if that card really is floating under the handkerchief in the same way that a mime performer makes it look like a balloon is lifting him up into the air. Give it the practice it deserves.

4

5

Chapter five
SHARK ATTACK

Fancy yourself as a cardshark? In this chapter you'll tackle some more ambitious card tricks. They require a bit more practice but don't worry – you don't have to have double-jointed fingers or hands quicker than the eye. The techniques described here can also be used to enhance the tricks you learned in the last chapter. And you'll get a chance to devise your own routine when you learn the final trick in this chapter – the Ambitious Card – get those creative juices flowing!

POKER IN THE EYE

This is a version of Big Deal from the last chapter, but with even less preparation. It's an impromptu demonstration of card cheating: you take a borrowed, shuffled pack and deal yourself a winning hand of cards. No preparation is needed, but you and your audience will need to have a reasonably advanced understanding of the game of poker.

The first thing you need to be familiar with are the winning hands. They are:

Royal flush: ....the ten, Jack ,Queen, King, ace of any suit.
Straight flush: ....five cards in sequence of the same suit.
Four of a kind: ....four cards of the same value.
Full house: ....any three of a kind plus a pair.
Flush: ....any five cards of same suit.
Three of a kind: ....three cards of same value.
Two pair: ....two cards of the same value and two cards of another.

The highest hand is the royal flush and the lowest is two pair, but apart from in the movies, one of the highest hands you'll normally see in a real game is a full house, so anyone who plays poker would be very impressed if you could deal yourself one of those, or even a flush, never mind four aces. And that's exactly what you do in this trick; you take a shuffled deck of cards and deal yourself a realistic winning hand at poker.

Here's the secret. Don't perform this as a challenge. Just do it casually during a game of cards, or after someone has watched you do a few tricks and asked the inevitable question, "Are you any good at cheating at cards?" Ask them to shuffle the cards. "Well, I suppose I could if I wanted. Tell you what: give them a shuffle." Take them back after the shuffle, saying, "If there are any jokers, we need to get rid of them for this; let me just check." Spread through the cards with their faces towards you. You're looking for the jokers, but you're also secretly looking for something else – a good poker hand. The poker hand you're looking for is any five cards which are already together in the deck and which make up a full house, a flush or two pair. No matter how much a deck is shuffled, it'll be an unusual and unlucky day if you can't find such a hand.

Now, you need to be paying attention to the cards to make this trick work, and you need to be really familiar with the hierarchy of poker hands; it's easy to miss a winning combination as you

quickly run through the cards. It's possible that you might find a great hand that's broken up by one indifferent card, for example a flush that's got an unwanted card right in the middle. If that's the case, just casually remove it and put it on top of the deck.

When and if you find the jokers, take them out too and place them on top of the deck. If they've already been removed, no problem; just comment that someone's already saved you the trouble. You can provide a little additional verbal misdirection as you scan the cards by asking the ambiguous question, "You sure you're playing with a full deck?" The spectator will usually assure you that they are, but the truth is that you might have set a little doubt in their mind; after all, it isn't as if people constantly check whether all the cards are present in a deck.

You need to do one more thing – when you spot a winning hand of cards, crimp the lower left corner of the card immediately to the left of it. Do this by bending it upwards with your left thumb **(1)**. In the photo I've crimped the card immediately above a full house made up of Queens and nines.

When you've run through the deck, square it up and take away any jokers you might have found. "Okay, the jokers are gone – let's start. Does everyone know how to play poker?" Failing a unanimous "No", you start your demonstration. "First the cards are cut." You cut your crimp to the bottom, which brings your winning

hand to the top. "Then they're dealt, left to right – dealer's is the last hand." Deal out five hands of five cards, dealing to yourself last. Turn over your hand and show which cards you're holding.

If it turns out to be a great hand, take all the credit for it and offer to repeat the demonstration. More often than not, it won't be so great. "As you can see – not a lot to play with. Here's where the cheating comes in." Gather up all the hands, being careful not to alter the position of any of the cards in them. Drop the hands back on top of the deck. Your crimp card is still on the bottom, so you can give the deck several cuts if you feel it might enhance the trick.

The last cut is made at the crimp, sending it back to the bottom. "Let's see what we can do – pay close attention to the right hand." Deal out five hands again and give a running commentary about where the cards are coming from. "I'm dealing regular cards to my opponents… all coming off the top of the deck. Watch when I deal my card, though: I'm going to deal myself one from the middle instead. There – did you see it?" Of course they didn't, because you took the card off the top just as you did with all the others.

Continue dealing hands and making exaggerated claims when it comes to dealing your own cards. Tell the spectators that they're coming from the middle, bottom or anywhere else except the top.

Name the hand that you spotted earlier; let's say it's a full house. "Now, it would be foolish to deal myself four aces; if you spot four aces in a hand, you know someone's probably been cheating. So what I'm going for is a full house. You can usually win with a full house – Queens and nines are what I'm looking for." When the deal's finished, turn over your hand. "Queens and nines: let's see what I got." Spectators should be suitably impressed with your hand.

NOTES

You'll see how similar this is to Big Deal, but the ability to be able to do it any time and without a set-up deck is well worth acquiring.

After the deal, I don't bother to show what the other hands of cards are. Luck might have put some very good cards there and I don't want to spoil my reputation by possibly losing the hand. There's an exception to this rule – if I've managed to find a really spectacular hand, like four of a kind, I'll risk showing all the other hands before revealing my own. And, naturally, in that case I'll take credit for any other interesting hands that are there, claiming that I was deliberately hooking everyone else in before delivering the sucker punch!

FIVE-A-SIDE POKER

The ultimate poker game. Just ten cards. The spectator has a free choice of five of them, leaving you with the other five. There are no draws, only winners. So why does he keep losing?

The Props

The secret of this scam lies in the ten cards you use. They're made up of three lots of Three of a Kind and one odd high-value card; for instance, three Jacks, three tens, three sevens and an ace **(1)**. The ace is marked on the back. I do this by scraping away a tiny bit of the design from the diagonally opposite corners of the card at the top left and bottom right **(2)**. It should be enough of a mark that you can identify it quickly but the spectators won't notice it.

First Deal

Begin by removing the necessary ten cards from the deck – your marked ace and three tens, three Jacks and three sevens. "Let me show you a swindle I learned from an old hustler. He only ever used ten cards and he'd bet professional poker players that they couldn't beat him. Here's what he did." Give the ten cards to a spectator.

"Everything seemed to be above board: he'd let you shuffle – so shuffle." The spectator does so. "Then he'd let you cut – so give the cards a cut." The spectator gives the packet a complete cut. "And he'd even let you deal – deal all the cards on to the table in a row."

The spectator deals the cards out into a row and you secretly note the position of your marked card **(3)**. I've pointed it out in the photo. In this instance it's fourth from your left, or seventh from left as the spectator sees it. "He wouldn't even pick the cards up in case you thought he was cheating – he just slid them across the table like this."

You're going to divide the cards up between you and the spectator, alternately sliding one to him and one to you, and you're going to make sure that he gets the ace. If the ace is at an even number as you look at the cards, you slide the first one to yourself, starting at the left end of the row as you look at it. If the ace is at an odd number, then slide the first card to the spectator.

Either way you ensure that the spectator gets the ace. The spectator turns his hand face-up; he might have two pair, but your hand will beat it with three of a kind. As long as he has the ace, he'll always lose against your hand. Take a look at the rank of poker hands listed in Poker in the Eye if you're not too familiar with the game.

Second Deal

"Don't worry. This game's harder than it looks." Gather up the ten cards and shuffle them. "He went one better than that: this time you shuffle, I'll cut, you choose – watch." Give the packet to the spectator. He shuffles and then hands the packet back to you. You spread it face-down between your hands and give it a cut, manoeuvring your marked ace so that it's somewhere near the top.

It can actually end up anywhere except the bottom of the packet. And then you hand the cards back to him. "Okay, I said you ☞

2

could choose. Take a look at the top card: you want to keep it or give it to me?" It's a genuine free choice. You ask him to look at each card one at a time and either deal it to himself or hand it to you. Because people think it's good strategy to have a high card, he'll usually choose to keep the ace rather than give it to you. As soon as he's dealt five cards to you, the game's over and the hands are shown. If he's got the ace – and you'll always know because it's marked – he'll lose.

Third Deal

This is the final phase. "I'm not sure why, but you keep dealing yourself bad cards. You should have had some of mine. Tell you what – this time you shuffle, cut and deal, but at the end we'll switch cards."

He shuffles, cuts and then deals the cards into two hands; one to you and one to him as per a regular game. You'll be able to see who's got the marked ace. If you've got it, you immediately say, "I said that you could, shuffle, cut and deal but that we'd switch cards. So let's swap the hands around." He gets your hand and you get his. And he's now got the ace, so he'll lose.

But if he deals the ace to his own hand you offer a different interpretation of switching cards: "Okay: you shuffled, cut and dealt, but now let's switch some cards – spread them out." He spreads out both hands of face-down cards on the table. This enables you to see exactly where the marked ace is in his hand. "Choose one of my cards and I'll choose one of yours." You both reach over to each other's hand. He pulls any card of yours out, and

you pull any card of his – any card, that is, except the ace. "Turn the card over." You both turn the cards over that you've just drawn from each other's hand. He might even beat you in this draw, which should please him. "Okay, then: let's see what else you've got." When you turn the hands over, once again he'll have lost.

NOTES

There are lots of ways of varying this trick. As you've seen, so long as the spectator has the ace, he'll lose. And if the ace ever ends up in your hand, all you need to do is come up with an excuse to switch some cards or the entire hand.

I sometimes like to bring in a different set of cards, saying, "You're not having much luck with this lot of cards; let's try some different ones." I have a King in the deck that's also marked and I take it out, together with another nine cards composed of three lots of three of a kind. The mix of new cards mean that it's difficult for the spectator to notice that, again, there's a wild card. As long as it's a high card, he'll always be tempted to take it.

And then, if I'm feeling really cruel, I take out yet another batch of cards. He shuffles them, drops the packet on top of the deck and deals out two hands. Looks completely fair – and yet he still loses. This is because I actually only took out nine cards. The odd card this time was on top of the rest of the deck. He shuffles the packet, not realizing that there are only nine cards. When he drops the packet on to the deck and deals out two hands, dealing to you first as normal, the tenth card falls to his hand – it's the odd card and he loses yet again. As they say; never give a sucker an even break!

FOUR SIGHT

In this demonstration you show how easily you can find any four of a kind or royal flush in the deck. Someone selects a card; the ten of hearts, for example. With a snap of the fingers the mate of that card, the ten of diamonds, turns face-up in the middle of the deck. And on the count of three, the remaining pair of tens suddenly appear. That's all four tens, and it took less time to find them than it took to read this paragraph.

This trick makes use of a pre-arranged stack of cards and a false shuffle. The routine isn't difficult to do, but it looks extremely impressive when performed snappily.

Here's the set up from the top of the deck down: face-down ten of hearts, face-up ten of clubs, face-up ten of spades, face-up ten of diamonds. The remainder of the deck is face-down underneath these four cards **(1)**. The first step is to convince your audience that the deck is in random order, and you do that by giving it a false shuffle: one which appears to mix up the cards, but actually brings your stack back to the top of the deck.

Begin with the deck held in the left hand for an overhand shuffle. The right hand cuts the lower half of the deck from underneath and lifts it up. The left thumb pulls off the top card of this right-hand packet but injogs it in so it sticks out a little towards you **(2)**. ☞

The right hand continues to shuffle cards on to the injogged card, but flush with all the other cards below. Continue shuffling until there are no more cards in the right hand. The result is that you have a card sticking out towards you, an injog, which lies directly above your set-up cards **(3)**. The right hand comes over the deck to give it a cut. The right thumb pulls up on the injogged card, creating a break below it while pushing it in flush with the rest of the top half of the deck **(4)**. The right hand lifts off all the cards above the break and cuts them to the bottom of the deck.

The end result is that although you appear to have given the deck a shuffle and a cut, your pre-arranged stack is still on top. You can use this false shuffle in any card routine which requires you to maintain what's known as a "top stock" of cards. You want to create the illusion that you can find any four of a kind in the deck, but in fact the spectator won't have any option in his apparently free choice; he'll choose the ten of diamonds no matter which card he points to.

The cards are already arranged for a very clever "force" devised by magician Henry Christ. You spread the cards from the left hand to the right hand, being careful to keep the top part of the deck bunched together so that the reversed cards can't be seen. Tell one of the spectators to "point to any one of the cards in the middle. Doesn't matter which one." He does **(5)**.

Break the spread so that the one they point to is the top card of the left-hand packet. Square up the right-hand packet by tapping it against the side of your left hand and then flip it over and drop it on top of the left-hand packet **(6)**. Spread the cards again as far down as the first face-down card, drawing attention to the face-up cards as you say, "You could have pointed to any one of these cards."

Separate the spread so that all the face-up cards are in your right hand. Thumb off the top face-down card of the left-hand packet, saying, "But you chose this one – take a look at it." Because of the ingenuity of Henry Christ's "force", the first face-down card

will be the ten of diamonds. Thumb it off the deck so that the spectator can take a look at it **(7)**.

I've exposed the reversed ten of hearts in this photo so that you can better understand the position of the set-up. It lies third from the top of the left-hand packet, but in actual performance you would be careful not to spread the packet too much or the spectator might spot it. While the spectator looks at his chosen card, you flip the right-hand packet face-down on top of the left-hand packet and then place the squared-up deck on the table. "This is an old gambler's trick. Let me show you: which card did

you choose? Turn it over." The spectator reveals the ten of diamonds. "Okay, ten of diamonds. Let me see if I can remember how to do this. I'm going to try to find the best mate of the ten of diamonds: that'll be the ten of hearts – watch." Snap your fingers over the deck on the table. "Doesn't look like much, does it? But look..." Spread the deck to reveal that the ten of hearts is now face-up in the middle **(8)**.

Pick up the deck, spread it between your hands and cut the ten of hearts to the top and place it face-up on the table. "That's two red tens. Let me see if I can find the two black tens." If you've ☞

followed the instructions, the two black tens are already on the bottom of the deck.

For the next phase, you need to move one of them to the top of the deck. Here's how you do it. Hold the deck in the left hand in overhand shuffle mode. The right hand cuts half the deck from underneath but the left fingers contact the bottom/face card of the deck, a black ten, and hold it in place as the cards above it are removed. The right hand then shuffles its cards on to the left packet. As you reach the last few cards of the right-hand packet, the left thumb peels them off one at a time so that the last card of the packet – one of the black tens – becomes the top card of the deck. You're almost ready for the finale.

Place the deck face-down in the left hand. Both hands are held about 18 inches apart at waist height. "Watch closely: it'll happen on the count of three." Count "One" and throw the deck from the left hand to the right, which catches it. On the count of "Two", throw the deck back to the left hand, except that this time you hold the top and bottom cards back **(9)**.

This is easy to do – just press down lightly with the right thumb on the top card of the deck and press upwards with the fingers on the bottom card of the deck while giving the hand a sideways jerk to send the rest of the deck flying from between them into the waiting left hand. The top and bottom cards stay in the right hand. Count "Three" while turning those two cards face-up and spreading them to show that they're the two black tens **(10)**. All four tens have now made a flashy and surprising appearance.

NOTES

Obviously you don't have to use the tens. You could use the same routine to produce four aces or any other four of a kind.

You can also change the trick slightly to produce different effects. For instance, set the cards up in this order: face-down Ace of spades, face-down King of spades, face-down Queen of spades, face-down Jack of spades, any card face-up, ten of spades face-up, followed by the rest of the deck face-down in any order.

Work the Henry Christ force as described. Because of the arrangement of cards, the spectator will select the ten of spades. Put the right-hand cards on top of the left-hand cards as before and place the deck on the table. Ask the spectator to show the card he's chosen, then say, "Ten of spades – not great, but any grifter could make it into a great hand. All they'd have to do is find your ten some good company – like this..." Snap your fingers over the deck and then spread it. There, face-up in the middle of the spread, are the Jack, Queen, King and Ace of spades. And you don't get much better than that!

ADVANCED CONTROL

This is a utility method of controlling the position of a card which depends upon sleight-of-hand rather than psychology or subtlety. A card is selected, remembered and replaced in the deck. With just two cuts, you can bring it to the top or bottom of the deck, ready to be produced in any number of ways.

1

2

"Take a card," you say in time-honoured tradition as you spread the deck from the left hand to the right. "Any one will do – quick as you like." This hurries the spectator along a little. When you're performing, you want to keep the pace up, so act as if you genuinely don't care which card they select – which in this case happens to be true. "You sure?" you say as soon as the spectator touches a card. Let him take it and then tell him to remember it. "Don't show me: that would make it too easy."

Divide the spread in two at the point from which the card was selected. The spectator remembers the card, shows it around to his friends, and then you extend the left-hand packet saying, "Just drop it back on top." **(1)** Don't give him too much time to think about this: just do it, and he'll follow your instructions and place the card back where you want it. Place the right-hand packet on top of his card but, as you do, secretly keep a break between the packets.

To do this, you just curl your left little finger around the side and on top of the bottom packet as you drop the top packet on to it **(2)**.

The fleshy pad of the little finger prevents the two packets closing all the way together. From the front, the packets seem to blend together perfectly. You now give the deck two cuts, and in doing so secretly move the selected card to the top of the deck.

For this "double undercut", begin by taking the deck from above in the right hand, fingers at the outer short end, thumb at the inner short end. The right thumb takes over the break. The left hand cuts off roughly half of the cards from the lower portion of the deck below the break **(3)**. You can see in the photo how the right thumb maintains the original break as this is done.

The left-hand packet of cards is now placed on top of the deck **(4)**. Then the left hand returns to a position under the deck, takes all the cards below the break and again places its packet on top of the deck **(5)**. The selected card is now the top card, and in the perfect position for you to reveal it.

Performed smoothly, this is a perfectly natural-looking move. It looks as if you've given the deck two quick cuts. You can add to the

belief that the selected card has been lost in the deck by giving the cards a false shuffle, as described in Four Sight earlier.

To do this, pick up the deck in preparation for an overhand shuffle. Let the upper half of the deck fall from the right hand into the waiting left hand. Now injog the next single card and shuffle the rest of the cards on to the top of that. Square the cards, converting the injog into a break. Cut the cards at the break and complete the cut. The selected card is now on top of the deck.

NOTES

The same control can be used to position the selected card on the bottom of the deck. When the card is replaced in the deck it will be jogged slightly over the right side of the bottom packet. The left little finger pushes up on the underside of the card and takes its break underneath it as the right-hand cards are placed on top. The deck is squared up with the selected card above the little finger break. After you make the double undercut, the selected card will be on the bottom of the deck rather than the top.

There's a saying in magic that if you know one good way to control a chosen card and a hundred ways to reveal it, then you know a hundred tricks: make the most of that theory.

THE DOUBLE LIFT

"Is this your card?" Unfortunately, the spectator tells you it's not. It appears you've made a bad mistake. Never mind: you take the wrong card and rub it on your sleeve and it magically changes into the right one!

This is achieved by means of a move known as a double lift, which is probably the most used – and sometimes over-used – move in card magic. In this example, you'll use it to change one card into another.

Let's assume someone's chosen a card and it's been replaced in the deck and apparently lost with a couple of cuts and a shuffle. During this sequence you've secretly brought the card to the top of the deck using the advanced control.

"You might think that your card's lost in the deck, but I can bring it to the top very quickly – very quickly indeed. All you need do is say the magic word." Pause a while as if waiting for the spectator to say something and, when they don't, repeat with some emphasis the instructions again. "All you need to do is say the magic word."

They'll assume that you're joking. Tell them that you aren't – you really do need them to say a magic word! "Any magic word will do. But because you selected the card, it's you who has to say it. Off you go!" There's fun to be had watching a fully-grown adult trying to come up with something which doesn't involve swearing. Let him say his word and then tell him, "No, you've got to say it with a bit more conviction." And make him say it a second time. "Better that time – and here's your card."

You now appear to turn over the top card, but this is where you perform the double lift sleight. Instead of turning over the top card, you turn over the top two cards as if they're a single one: With the deck held in the left-hand dealing grip, the right hand extends its forefinger and pulls up on the cards at the inner end of the deck **(1)**. The fleshy pad of the forefinger catches the top card and drags it upwards. Unknown to the spectators, the pad of your finger also contacts a second card and drags it upwards too **(2)**.

Keep pulling upwards on the two cards until they close up together. You'll find that if you curl the first joint of the right forefinger inwards, the cards will naturally slide together and line themselves up as one. They're held by the right thumb on top and the right forefinger underneath. Drag them both to the side of the deck, holding them there briefly **(3)**. You can clamp them in place against the top of the deck with the left thumb and move the right hand away at this point if you want.

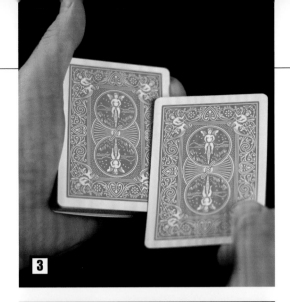

When you're ready to turn the cards over, grip them again with the right thumb and forefinger at the inner right corner. The left thumb moves out of the way and the right hand flips the two cards face-up on to the deck. The cards hinge over on their long side. This turning action has to be done in one smooth movement and you should do it so that the two cards land injogged at the inner end of the deck **(4)**. That's the first part of the move; you've turned over the top two cards together so that they appear to be one single card. Draw attention to the face of the visible card, saying, "And there it is – your card!" Actually it's the wrong card and the spectator won't usually waste much time before telling you so.

"I knew you weren't really into that magic word business," you reply. You turn the double card back face-down on to the deck. ☞

7

The injog makes this easier. The right hand just takes the two aligned cards at the inner right corner. Drag them to the right of the deck and then flip the pair over **(5)**.

Again the cards hinge on their long side. This time the cards land square on the deck. Thumb off the top card into the right hand. Take it at the inner right corner and rub the face-down card on your left sleeve as if trying to wipe the face off it **(6)**. "Looks like I've got to do all the work round here! What was the name of your card then?"

As soon as the spectator has named his selection, use the right third finger to give the card a snap. "That should do it." Turn the card over to reveal that it's now transformed into the chosen card **(7)**.

NOTES

The double lift is one of the most important moves in card magic. To do it well, you must always remember to handle the two cards as if they really are just one single card. At first you'll find it difficult to keep the cards aligned with each other, but it'll become easier with practice. When performed properly, the move is absolutely undetectable. Even professional magicians can't tell whether an expert is actually handling two cards or one. It's even possible to handle three cards as one when you get good!

The key to the move is lightness of touch. Try to appear casual as you flip the cards over on to the deck. As far as the spectators are concerned, you're simply turning over a single playing card – nothing more, nothing less. Too many would-be magicians make the move look like a move! Remember you're supposedly dealing with a single playing card, not a paving slab!

STABBED IN THE DECK

The spectator tries her hand at finding a selected card. You tell her that if she takes a joker and stabs it into the middle of the deck, she'll place that joker right next to the previously chosen card. Funnily enough, she believes you.

However, when she tries the trick she misses. Neither of the cards either side of the joker proves to be the right one. The surprise comes when she turns over the joker. It's magically changed into the selected card!

This trick uses the double lift to make one card change to another while the spectator's holding it. It starts like the conventional card trick with the spectator choosing a card. She remembers and replaces it in the deck – you control it to the top using the advanced control move. Let's assume that she chose the King of hearts.

"I've been finding your cards all night. It's about time that you did some of the work. Don't worry; it's easy." Use the double lift to turn over the top two cards of the deck as one. Point to the card that's now face-up on top, saying, "Is that your card? No? Good." Name the card – let's assume in this case that it's the Joker. Flip the two cards over and thumb the top face-down card into the right hand. Be careful not to show its face because this is the

selected card. Tell the spectator, "Here's what I want you to do – take the joker, keep it face-down, and stab it somewhere into the middle of the deck. Don't think about it – just do it. Use your intuition and don't worry about being vicious!" You hand her the face-down card and then hold the deck face-up in the left hand so that she can thrust the card into it at its outer short end **(1)**.

She'll stick the card in face-down somewhere in the middle of the deck. Tell her not to let go of the card as you spread the deck from hand to hand **(2)**. Divide the deck at the face-down card. Then ask her whether her chosen card is the top one of the left-hand packet. She'll say no. "So it must be the one on the other side?" Show her the face card at the bottom of the right ☞

spread of cards. Again she'll say no. Look her straight in the eyes, asking, "What card did you choose then?" When she tells you it was the King of hearts, reply, "So what card did you think you were holding?" She'll usually scream when she finds that she's been holding that card all along **(3)**.

NOTES

This isn't a difficult trick to perform but it requires good management of the spectator. Don't pick someone who looks as though they might try to spoil the trick by being difficult and maybe taking a premature look at the card in their hand.

An alternative, once you've shown the face-up joker after the double lift, is apparently to push it face-down into the deck yourself, square the cards up and then spread the deck face-up across the table. Push out the face-down card together with the face-up cards either side of it. When she's denied that either of the face-up cards is hers, ask her to turn over the face-down card. She'll freak out.

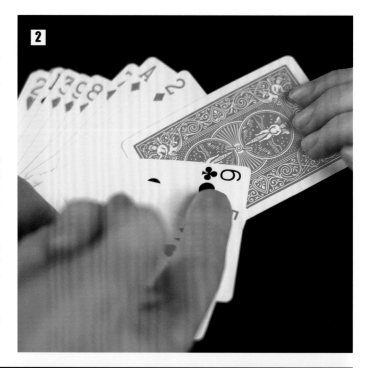

AMBITIOUS CARD

A classic of magic in which the spectator's selected card rises to the top of the deck again and again. And again. Even when the cards are in his own hands.

The Ambitious Card plot is a standard of magic and most magicians have their own favourite version. I'll break the trick down into different stages so that you can learn each phase separately and then combine them together in any way that suits you.

The First Rise

Spread the cards face-down between your hands and ask a spectator to choose one. As they take it, separate the deck at that point and square up both halves. They look at, remember and replace their card on top of the lower left-hand pile.

You shuffle off a single card from the right-hand pile on to the top of the left, injogging it as in the advanced control described earlier, then shuffle the rest of the right-hand cards on top of that. Now, rather than pushing up with the right thumb to make the break below the injogged card, you push down to make the break above

it. Continue with the double undercut. This time the selected card has ended up second from the top.

"This isn't one of those tricks in which you take a card and I tell you what it is. In this trick you take a card and you tell me what it is. No, really: what was your card?" When the spectator announces the name of his card – let's say it's the Jack of clubs, say, "I don't believe it! The Jack of clubs? That's the most ruthlessly ambitious card in the deck: it's never happy unless it's on top. Look..." Flip over the top card of the deck in the same way that you'd do a double lift and then flip it face-down again as you say, "It's not here."

Flip the entire deck over in the left hand, displaying the bottom/face card while saying, "And it's not here." Turn the deck face-down again. "But if I snap my fingers, watch what happens." Snap your right finger and thumb and then do a double lift. The Jack of clubs now appears as if it's the top card of the deck. ☞

1

The Second Rise

"I'll do that again," you say. "The first time's always too fast." Flip the double card face-down on to the deck. Thumb off the top card as though it's the Jack you just displayed and take it in the right hand. Insert it into the deck from the inner short end **(1)**. Push the card flush. "The Jack goes into the middle, but if I snap my fingers it claws its way right back to the top of the pile again." Turn over the top card to show that the Jack's back.

The Third Rise

This sequence uses a move called "Tilt", invented by the late Ed Marlo, a Chicago card expert. At the moment the Jack is still face-up on top of the deck. Flip it face-down and thumb it off into the right hand. As you're about to put the Jack into the middle of the deck as you did before, you show its face once more time. Your right hand raises the card so that the spectators are now in no doubt that you are actually holding the Jack of clubs **(2)**. "Watch Jack jump."

As the spectators look at the Jack, the left hand prepares for the tilt move. Lower the left hand towards you and push the top card

over a little with your thumb. Pull it back again, but retain a break below it with your little finger. Move the left thumb so that it lies along the left side of the deck. This will allow the top card to pop up into the tilt position; this is one in which a large break is held between the inner end of the top card and the rest of the deck.

Always keep the right side of the deck turned away from the audience. If you keep the surface of the top card parallel with the floor, the spectators won't suspect the gap at the rear of the deck. It takes a knack to learn to set up the tilt position with one hand, but once mastered it only takes a moment and the showing of the Jack provides all the cover you need.

Hold the deck just below chest height. The right hand lowers the Jack and appears to push it into the middle of the deck as before, but really pushes it into the gap and along the top of the main portion of the deck **(3 & 4)**.

From the spectator's point of view the Jack appears to be going into the middle of the deck, but really it ends up second from the top. Push the Jack flush with the rest of the deck, then give it a shake and, as you do so, allow the break between the deck ☞

and the top card to collapse. Snap your fingers and then make a double lift, turning the top two cards over as one to reveal that the Jack seems to have somehow climbed back to the top again.

Final Rise

Flip the double card face-down and thumb the top one off into the right hand. "Maybe you'll see how it works if I use fewer cards. Just cut some off and leave me about half the deck." The spectator believes you've got the Jack face-down in the right hand. He reaches over to the deck and cuts off half of the cards **(5)**.

You now insert the right-hand card into the middle of the cards you're holding in the left hand **(6)**. Make it look exactly the same as your previous handling. "Okay: not many cards here. Watch Jack jump back to the top again." Snap your fingers and then proudly flip over the top card of the packet. The Jack isn't there. Act surprised. "Hmm. Maybe he went to the bottom, then..." Flip the packet over. No Jack there either. Spread the cards face-up between the hands as if searching for the Jack. "Wait a minute – I know what happened. He didn't jump to the top of my cards: he jumped to the top of yours!" Ask the spectator to turn over the top card of the packet he's holding. "There you go!" **(7)**.

NOTES

If you want to elaborate on the routine you can add more phases by using some of the tricks and moves you've already learned.

For instance, begin the trick with a version of the Card Counter routine. Don't have the card signed; perform the routine as a way of finding a chosen card in the conventional way; the spectator looks at his card, replaces it in the deck and you use your credit card to find it. Then you tell him that not only is the card radioactive, but it can also perform a quantum leap in the deck. You shuffle his card into the deck as you talk, but in fact you use a false shuffle to bring the card to the second position from the top of the deck and then perform the First Rise phase of the Ambitious Card routine.

Or use a handling of Stabbed in the Deck as follows. Let's imagine that you've secretly brought the selected card, the Jack of clubs, to the top of the deck. Do a double lift to show that the top card isn't the one you're looking for. Turn the double card face-down, thumb it off and hand it to the spectator, saying, "But if you wave that card over the deck, the Jack will appear on the top."

The spectator waves the card he's holding and you then turn over the top card of the deck. It still isn't the Jack. Flip the deck over, saying, "Maybe it went to the bottom, then." It isn't there either. Spread the face-up cards as if looking for the missing Jack of clubs. Then, as if an idea's suddenly dawned on you, turn to the spectator and say, "I know what happened: the Jack jumped too far – look!" He'll be amazed to find that he's actually holding on to the jumping Jack.

The Ambitious Card is a showstopper of a routine and the more you know about card magic, the more you can personalize this trick and devise a routine that's unique to you. Get thinking!

7

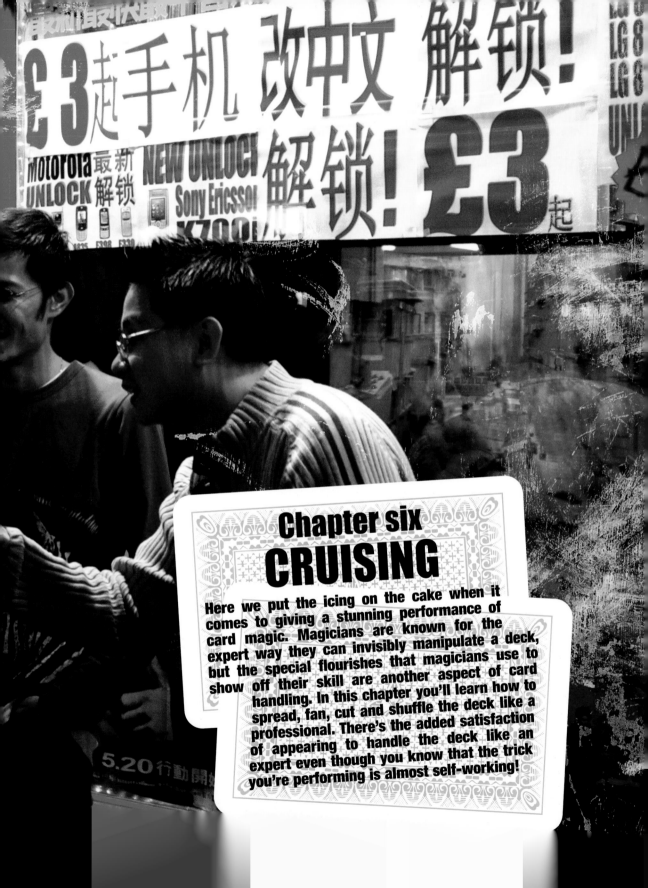

Chapter six
CRUISING

Here we put the icing on the cake when it comes to giving a stunning performance of card magic. Magicians are known for the expert way they can invisibly manipulate a deck, but the special flourishes that magicians use to show off their skill are another aspect of card handling. In this chapter you'll learn how to spread, fan, cut and shuffle the deck like a professional. There's the added satisfaction of appearing to handle the deck like an expert even though you know that the trick you're performing is almost self-working!

PRESSURE FAN

The benchmark of a good card manipulator is to be able to spread the deck in an even fan so that the indices of all the cards are showing. Here's how you can add this impressive flourish to your card work.

The advantage of the pressure fan above other fanning techniques is that it works with most types of playing card.

If you're really interested in card magic, then avoid really cheap decks of cards and, equally, expensive-looking cards which have been plastic-coated. The best cards are the type used in casinos: they wear well and don't grow thick and dog-eared with use.

To make a pressure fan, start with the deck in the right hand, with the thumb at the inner short end and the fingers at the outer short end. Hold out the left hand and press the lower part of the deck against the left fingers **(1)**.

You're now going to fan the deck in a clockwise direction. To do this, bend the deck between the right fingers and thumb. Now move the right hand in a clockwise direction with the right thumb acting as a pivot for the action. As the right hand moves, it allows the cards to spring, under pressure, from the right hand and on to the left. They're left behind gradually in a neat arc as the right hand moves. The left thumb is kept out of the way.

At this point it's only the firm presence of the right hand that prevents the cards from falling to the floor. When the right hand has reached the lowest point of its arc, the left thumb clamps the deck to the left hand **(2)**.

The right hand can now move away – you should be left with a perfect fan. From the front, the indices of virtually all the cards should be visible **(3)**. To close the fan, the right forefinger contacts the lower right edge of the fan and pushes it back in an anti-clockwise direction until all the cards are squared in the left hand.

NOTES

The pressure fan looks flashy. It's designed to impress the spectators but, as with all the flourishes in this chapter, you should be careful how you use it. It shows that you're familiar and comfortable with the deck, but if you over-use moves like this you risk being looked upon as a show-off.

Sometimes flourishes can make a routine look elegant, but at other times they can actually detract from the magic: they make the tricks look as if they're purely the result of manual dexterity rather than something more esoteric. In fact, there are magicians who deliberately fake being clumsy with the cards so their audiences don't believe their tricks could result purely from sleight-of-hand and, therefore, their magic seems all the more mysterious.

It's basically a judgement call, but a really important one, and you should seriously consider what fits your own personal style and the kind of impression you want to leave your audience with.

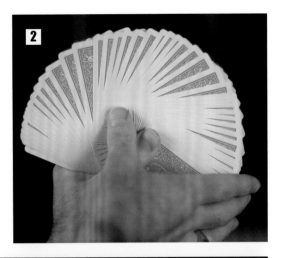

RIBBON SPREAD AND TURNOVER

This flourish is the epitome of cool – you've probably seen it in the movies, where the star takes the deck and spreads it face-down with a swift smooth sweep of the hand in a perfect line across the table. Then, with equal ease, he starts at one end and with a wave-like motion flips the entire deck face-up.

of the spread **(3)**. Maintain the contact and move the card to the left. The whole deck is tipped over this way, the single card riding the top of the spread like a surfer on a wave **(4)**. Continue moving the single card to the left until the entire spread is face-up on the table **(5)**.

NOTES

You can use this manoeuvre in several of the routines described in this book; in fact it fits in anytime you want to enforce your image as a master card sharp.

To perform the flourish, you need a deck of cards that spreads easily – an old dog-eared deck won't do. And you'll need a cloth-covered surface to perform on; the baize of a card or pool table is ideal but the tablecloth in a restaurant will work just as well.

Start with the deck face-down in the left hand. The thumb is at the inner end of the deck and the fingers at the outer end. The forefinger is positioned on the right long side of the deck **(1)**.

Place the deck flat on the table, apply some pressure and draw it to the left. The table cloth will drag the cards out from the bottom of the deck in a line. The forefinger controls the escape of the cards, letting them out one by one until the deck is spread in an even line **(2)**.

There's a knack to this, so start slowly and then speed up as you practice. Take the top card of the spread in the right hand. Slide the edge of this single card under the right edge of the spread and lever it upwards. Note how the edge of the single card contacts the edge

SPRINGING THE CARDS

This is the classic attention-getting magician's flourish – spraying the cards noisily over a distance from one hand and the other. It isn't easy; it takes practice. But you won't half feel cool when you can do it!

As I mentioned in the introduction, I'm left-handed. And because most of the readers of this book will be right-handed, I had to learn to do all the tricks in this book the right-handed way otherwise the photographs wouldn't have made much sense.

Well, there's one trick I still can't do right-handed, and it's this one: so I hope you'll indulge me, because what follows is a description of how I perform this flourish. You right-handers will have to reverse the left/right instructions to learn the trick.

Now you see what I've had to put up with for all these years! I'm going to start with the deck held in the left hand, fingers on the outer short end and thumb on the inner short end and then spring the cards from the left hand into the waiting right hand. I'm also putting pressure on the cards by squeezing the thumb and fingers together. You can see the cards starting to bend in the photo **(1)**.

With the left hand palm-down so that the cards are about nine or so inches above the right hand, I then apply more pressure to the cards, squeezing the left fingers and thumb together. If you do this correctly, you'll find that you can allow the cards to squirt free of the left hand. They slip off the left thumb and shoot in a continuous and unbroken stream to be caught in the right hand **(2)**.

There's a knack to this, particularly in allowing the cards to slip off the thumb rather than both the fingers and the thumb, which will usually just result in them spraying all over the place. Once you've mastered it, you can increase the distance

between your hands by moving the top hand higher.

Also, try holding the right hand close the body and the left hand a little further away. You then spring the card towards the body and the right hand. You can use your body as a barrier to stop the cards bouncing out of the right hand and falling. You might find it useful to bring your hands back closer together as the last of the cards leave the left hand **(3)**. One distinctive characteristic of this flourish is the cool sound of the cards squirting out of your hand one after the other – do this flourish in a bar and you'll soon have everyone's attention.

NOTES

Before trying to squirt the cards over too great a distance, first concentrate on mastering the release of the cards from the left hand. Try to make the springing of the cards controlled and even – it's not a quick burst of flying cards that you're trying to achieve; it's a longer, steady stream.

Although I let the cards escape from the thumb of my left hand, many other magicians prefer to let the cards escape from their fingers and spring from the hand in a forward motion. It's purely a matter of personal preference.

With practice, you'll find that you can hold your hands further and further apart. You can play with variations: for example, starting with the hands close together, start to spring the cards and then move them apart so that the river of cards gets larger and then, just as the last of the cards has left your hand, bring your hands quickly back together, square the deck and you're ready to begin your performance. ✋

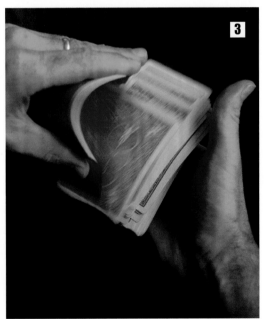

RIFFLE SHUFFLE

This is how gamblers shuffle cards. They split the deck into two and riffle the halves together, finishing it off with a fancy "waterfall" flourish. Master this shuffle and it makes you look like you really know what you're doing with a deck.

The riffle shuffle can be used to great effect in any gambling routine. Start with the deck held vertically in the left hand. The lower short end of the deck rests on the curled fingers, the thumb is on the top end of the deck and the cards are facing towards your right. Holding back the top half of the deck with the left thumb at the upper end **(1)**, allow the bottom half of the deck to fall on to the waiting right fingers **(2)**. Push upwards on the bottom end of the bottom packet with the left fingers, pivoting it on the right fingers so that it flips over and up with the right thumb taking hold of it so that it's in exactly the same grip as the left-hand packet **(3)**.

The fingers of each hand hold the lower part of the packets. You'll find that if you curl the fingers tightly under the cards it helps

to get a good firm grip. At the same time, the thumbs pull back on the upper end of the packets, bending them backwards in preparation for the shuffle **(4)**. To shuffle the packets together, turn them towards a horizontal position and allow the inner ends to simultaneously slip free of the thumbs in a riffling action **(5)**.

The two packets interlace. Keep riffling the cards together as evenly as you can until both thumbs have no cards left. At this stage you could push the two halves together to reform the deck; however, there's an additional and even more flourishy finish to the shuffle called the "waterfall".

To do the waterfall you flex the cards upwards into an arch by pressing inwards and up with your curled fingers. The thumbs press down on top of the arch to stop the cards unweaving **(6)**. At this point the cards are under a lot of pressure. If you now gradually relax your fingers downwards and outwards, the cards will cascade down and fall together with an impressive rushing sound **(7)**. When the cards have fallen just push the cards together and square up the deck.

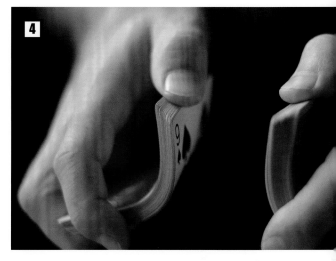

NOTES

This is a very professional-looking shuffle and immediately marks you out as someone familiar with cards and card play. Although it appears that the shuffle mixes the cards thoroughly, you can include an element of card control very easily. Let's imagine you know the selected card is on top of the deck. You want to shuffle the cards but you don't want to lose track of it. All you do is allow the top card to fall last during the shuffle. If you've followed the instructions, the selected card will be on top of the left-hand packet.

When you riffle the cards together, riffle the left-hand packet more slowly allowing its top card to fall last. This ensures that the top card of the deck will remain on top even after the shuffle. Two quick riffle shuffles in succession should convince anyone you've thoroughly mixed the deck, but leaves you in a position to perform whichever particular revelation of their card you care to.

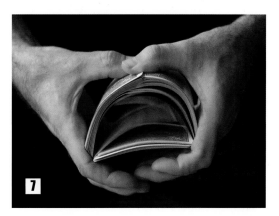

ONE-HANDED CUT

Here's another fancy way of manipulating the deck which gives the impression of great manual dexterity. In this flourish, you hold the deck up and give it a one-handed cut. No one's going to want to play poker with you once they've seen you do this.

The one-handed cut is sometimes known as the Charlier Cut, named after a 19th-century card manipulator. There's no doubt that Charlier was an outstanding card manipulator, although there's no real evidence that he invented this particular method of cutting the cards.

You can use either hand to perform the move; let's describe this one for the lefties again. Hold the deck face-down between the fingers on one long side and the thumb on the other. You'll notice that the left forefinger is curled below the deck **(1)**.

The thumb now relaxes pressure on its side of the deck and allows a break to open up, splitting the deck roughly in two **(2)**. Let this lower portion of the deck fall away from the thumb, hinging at the fingers side, to drop on to the palm. Its fall is controlled by the forefinger underneath which then pushes the far side of the lower packet upwards towards the thumb. The forefinger continues to push it up towards you until it clears the edge of the upper packet **(3)**. This results in the upper packet dropping on to the back of your forefinger.

Uncurl the left forefinger from beneath the deck, allowing what was the upper packet to drop on to your palm, then push down with the left thumb on top of the other packet, snapping the halves of the deck together **(4)**.

If you now curl the forefinger back under the cards you will find that you can push the entire deck back up to its original position between

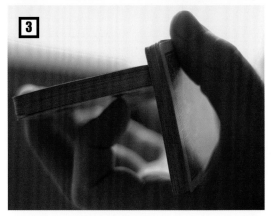

the thumb and fingers **(5)**. That's it – you've cut the deck and completed the cut with one hand in no more than a second.

If you're feeling really flash, why not practice it with both hands and then using half the deck in each simultaneously? **(6)**. The one-handed cut can be used in any routine that uses a key card. Cutting the deck repeatedly looks as if you're mixing the cards, but in fact the cuts do nothing to separate your key card from the spectator's selection.

NOTES

As mentioned earlier, flourishes are great for displaying your dexterity but they can detract from the magic, and they can make it look as if you're showing off: after all, you are! An occasional one can be used to great effect, though, especially in gambling routines where you're apparently demonstrating the grifter's tricks of the trade. It's perfectly legitimate to perform one of these fancy cuts if you're talking about seeing a gambler or card cheat doing it.

In this case the flourish illustrates how clever the cheat was and it looks a lot less like you're just trying to be flash.

SHOOTING STAR

This is a great, eye-popping climax to any trick where you discover a chosen card. You give the cards a simple cut and, as the halves of the deck are placed together, the selected card suddenly shoots out across the table.

This is a simple method for a showy revelation. Ideally, it should be performed on a smooth, polished table, the slick surface allowing the card to spin across it much further than a cloth-covered surface would. Let's assume that a card's been selected and replaced and you've controlled it to the bottom of the deck by means of a crimp.

The right hand holds the deck with the thumb on the inner long edge and the fingers on the outer long edge, and the left hand adjusts to a similar grip, but underneath the deck. The left little finger curls in and contacts the face of the selected card. From this position, it's easy for it to press on the face of the bottom card and push it to the right so that it projects for about an inch **(1)**.

The right fingers hide the projecting card from the spectators. The right hand holds the deck as the left hand lets go, turns over

3

and cuts off a portion of cards from the top of the deck, carrying them forward and placing them on the table **(2)**. The right hand now moves forward as if to place its packet on top of the one on the table, but as it does the right third finger starts to pull back on the projecting card, putting it under pressure **(3)**.

Just before you place the right packet on top of the packet on the table, allow the bottom card to spring forward off the right third finger **(4)**. It'll shoot and spin a considerable way across the table.

NOTES

This is a really surprising move; it's totally unexpected when the card pops out of the deck and shoots towards the spectators.

It makes an impressive flashy finish to any trick in which you are producing four of a kind; say, aces; just control the last ace to the bottom of the deck and have it propel itself across the table as you give the cards a cut.

4

Chapter seven
MIND MAGIC

The ultimate arena for magic is the mind. When you perform a magic trick the audience is baffled but they know that their amazement is the result of your skills. However, when you present a mind-reading trick, audiences seem to take it at face value – they genuinely want to believe that such a thing is possible. Be prepared for that – remember that magic doesn't happen in your hands; it happens in the mind of the audience. And, after you've performed a few tricks from this chapter, don't be surprised if people start queuing up to have their palms read!

THROWAWAY PREDICTION

An anywhere, any time miracle of prophecy in which you predict which one of half a dozen objects on a table someone will choose.

This stunt uses a clever force. Once you understand the principle, it can be used in various ways. Here, it's used to make a spectator choose a specific object from the six on the table. As well as half a dozen different items, you'll also need a pen and paper to make your prediction with.

Let's assume you're at a party. You tell everyone you want to try an experiment and you start to clear the table before putting six different objects on it: a glass, bottle, ashtray, matches, cigarette lighter, fork. It doesn't actually matter what they are.

Write the name of one of the objects on a piece of paper without anyone seeing, fold it up and give it someone to hold. "Don't read it yet," you say. We'll imagine that you've written, "You will choose the matches" on the paper. "This isn't magic. It's psychology. It's the kind of thing the military use to instil obedience in their soldiers. So I want you to follow my instructions very closely and very quickly: what happens might just surprise you."

Pick out someone to help you and then ask them to look over the objects. Call out the items one at a time. "When I snap my fingers I want you to pick up two of the objects immediately, one in each hand. I'll point to one of them and you just get rid of it: just hand it to one of the guys here as quickly as you can. Place the other one back on the table. Got it?" Assuming he's understood you, snap your fingers and he picks up two objects. It doesn't matter which two he picks; you point to one and tell him to throw it to one of the other spectators.

However, if he picks up the matches, the object you've predicted, you always point to the other object and he always puts the matches back on the table. This is the only important thing you need to remember. There are now five objects on the table. One's been eliminated. "Okay: my turn." You quickly pick up any two objects – any except the matches – and hold them up one in each hand for the spectator to see. "Point to the one you want me to throw away. The other goes back on the table."

He points to one, you throw it to the other spectators and put the remaining object back on the table. "Quick: again. Pick up two

objects." He does, and again you point to one and he throws it away and puts the remaining object back on the table.

Once again, if one of the objects he chose was the matches, make sure you point to the other one. There are now three objects on the table. Pick up the two that aren't matches. He points to one and you throw it away, placing the other one back down. Ask him to take the last two objects, one in each hand. As he does, you turn your back on him, casually noting in which hand he takes the matches as you do so. "Okay: one last time. Throw away the object in your..." pause here for effect and then say, "...right hand. What are you left with?" In fact, you already know where the matches are, so you can safely tell him to throw the object away that's in the other hand, but if you get the timing right on this people will think that you turned away before he picked up the objects and therefore couldn't have had any idea which hand held which object.

Tell him to put the last object behind his back. Turn around to face him. He's holding the matches out of sight, a move that again psychologically helps give the impression that you're not sure which object he's left with. "Did you notice what I was doing? You hardly had time to think – you picked up two objects, chose one, threw the other away. Which object are you left with?" He reveals the matches. Try to look surprised. Then ask the spectator who's holding your prediction to read it out. It says, "You will choose the matches."

NOTES

As previously mentioned, the force used in this routine, devised by British magician Roy Baker, can be used in many different ways. Here are just a couple.

First, you don't have to write your prediction down. You could secretly attach a sticker with the words "You will choose this" written on it to the bottom of any one of the objects. That's the object you avoid. Get the spectator to turn the final object over to reveal your secret message. All the people holding the discarded objects will now turn them over too, thinking they must all have a similar sticker. They'll be amazed that the chosen object is the only one.

Take half a dozen envelopes and secretly mark one of them by nicking it at the corner with your nail. You mark it just enough so that you can tell it apart from the others. To perform the routine, borrow a banknote and seal it in the marked envelope. You put pieces of paper into the other envelopes.

Go through the force procedure and this time have the spectators set light to the discarded envelopes in an ashtray, or, if you're in an office, you could put them through a shredding machine. Naturally you avoid discarding the marked envelope at every turn. Whoever loaned you the money will be relieved to find that the last envelope chosen contains their cash.

Apply your imagination and see what other interesting variations you can come up with. 🖐

GRAPHOLOGY

Graphology is the analysis of a person's handwriting to reveal their character. In this routine, you accurately analyze the writing of four total strangers.

You can present this trick in an informal setting with a few people gathered around a table, but it's also big enough to include in a larger show. In this example, we'll assume that you have a party-sized audience in front of you.

You'll also need four pieces of paper and four envelopes. The pieces of paper are ordinary but three of the envelopes have been marked by placing nail nicks at their edges (1). The nail nicks have been highlighted in black in the photo. The first envelope is marked at the top edge, the second on the right side and the third on the left side. You can identify the fourth envelope by the fact that it's the only one that isn't marked.

Notice too that the nail nicks are all marked on the flap side of the envelopes, so you know which side to look for them on. Hand the envelopes out to four people, making sure you know who has which one. It's easiest to think of handing the envelopes out to your spectators from left to right, with envelope number one being given to the left-most volunteer and so on round to the right.

Hand them each a sheet of paper and a pen and tell them that in a minute you're going to play a game of word association. You'll mention three words and then you want them to think of any single word which comes to mind and write it down on their piece of paper.

Then they're to fold the paper in half and put it inside the envelope. They should try not to let anyone see the word they've written. When they understand this, you start the word association game.

"Listen carefully. Here are the words. 'Apple'. That's the first word. Here's the next word: 'Sun'. And here's the last word: 'Blue'. Apple, sun, blue. Now I'm going to turn around and I want you to write down any word that comes to mind. Okay, do it now." You turn your back to the volunteers and they write down their words.

Wait a few moments and then tell them to fold their papers and put them into the envelopes and then seal them. Then they pass them to a completely independent person who mixes the envelopes up.

"Tell me when you've done that." You turn around and take the envelopes and now you begin to spin a yarn. "We're playing a game of word association. You know, it's amazing how much you can tell about a person by what word they think of." Take one of the envelopes and open it, take out the paper and read the word. "Not to mention the way they write it..." Don't show the paper to anyone else.

As you open the envelope, you note the position of your marking. This tells you which person wrote the word inside. You're about to give a character reading about that person based, supposedly, on their handwriting and their choice of word. In actual fact, you have a distinct and unfair advantage because you know who that person in your audience is. Take a sneaky look and try to work out what kind of a person they are. Let's assume this one is young, fashionable and with her boyfriend, with whom she's very tactile.

Here's the kind of thing you could say. "Interesting choice of word. Even more interesting is the way it's written; some people use their best handwriting, some use capitals, some I can hardly read, but this word is written very clearly, almost like filling in a form. The lines and curves tell me a lot. This is a person who likes to be in control but also has a soft side; likes to be the boss but also likes affection.

"It shows a neat and orderly character, youthful, too. Probably considers themselves to be quite trendy: and, I reckon, quite possibly in love at the moment. Let me try to go a bit further. It's definitely written by a female. I reckon she'd be fashionable and quite pretty – and, unfortunately, already in a relationship. Just remind me again which of you wrote words down: can you all put your hands up, please?" The four people raise their hands.

As soon as they do, everyone will be looking to see which one is the young pretty fashionable girl you've been talking about. Pick her out of the four people, saying, "I think it could very well be you. What word did you write?" She calls out her word and you immediately turn the paper around to show that you're correct. "One down, three to go. Let's try a second word."

Open another envelope and again note the marking. Again, this tells you which of your volunteers wrote the word. "Let's try this differently. I want everyone who wrote something to keep a straight poker face. I'm going to show you the word." Turn the paper around and reveal the word to the audience. You can get some fun out of this no matter what word has been written. Remind everyone that you called out three words at the beginning: apple, sun and blue. Now read out the word that's written on the paper.

It might be something that follows your words in a logical fashion or it might be something totally out of left field. Whichever it is, make the most of it. For example: "So I called out 'apple', 'sun' and 'blue' and that made one of you guys think of 'wine'. Now, why would anyone think of 'wine'? Perhaps there's some obvious connection between wine and those three words that I'm not making? Is it because you're holding a glass of wine? Fancy some wine? Or maybe it's your answer to everything? Are we looking at a connoisseur or someone who needs professional help?"

You're just having a bit of fun with the reading, but now you pretend to get a little more serious, as during the above you've sized up the spectator who wrote the word. Let's assume it's a middle-aged man. Your reading might go something like this: "So, 'wine': a sophisticated drink, and so possibly written by a sophisticated person; someone who appreciates the finer things in life. Probably someone with a little worldly wisdom: not someone who's immature, someone more experienced in life. And written in a very masculine hand; definitely written by a man... and I think that man was you." At this point, look directly at the guy who wrote the word.

He admits that it was indeed him; that leaves two words left. You open both envelopes and take out both sheets of paper, mentally noting which sheet belongs to which of the two remaining volunteers. Ask the two people to raise their hands for a moment and then ask them their occupations. "Okay – retail manager and financial analyst. That'll give me something to work on."

You could end the trick right here, but it wouldn't be all that effective. It would be more likely to look like the trick that it is, rather than genuine psychology. You have to convince everyone that you're using the information the volunteers have given you to assess the two words on the papers. Read the words to the audience, "'Door' and 'lemon'. Two different words and two different people. The first is very bold, very solid: capital letters again. The second is written in flowing script – large loops, denoting honesty – while the straight lines of the capitals show strength of personality. Let me try one more thing." Look at the volunteers and say, "I want you both to name a colour. You first: when I snap my fingers, call out a colour. And now you. Any colour: just call it out."

It doesn't matter what colours they call out: this is just pure showmanship to help give the impression that you're somehow using psychological means again to determine who wrote which word. Pause dramatically, then bring the trick to a close by handing each sheet to the correct person, "'Door' is yours, I believe. And that means that you're the lemon!" You're right on both counts.

NOTES

This routine depends on convincing blarney. You have to be able to make numerous general statements about people's character after taking just a brief look at them and then tie these statements into your routine. A good way to practice is to just sit on a train or in a cafe and look at the people around you. What would you say about them if they were helping out with the routine?

Magicians call this kind of bogus character analysis "cold reading" and there are lots of books written about it. It's the main tool used by many so-called psychics. Essentially, it's about making very general and mostly flattering statements to people who subjectively believe that they apply very specifically to them.

If you look at this routine, you'll see that you actually tell the spectators very little, yet they'll be drawn in because they really do believe that you're analyzing what their word and handwriting might reveal about them. And because you only ever say reasonably flattering things about them – being strong or fashionable or attractive, for example – they'll find it hard to disagree with anything you say! It's part of the magic which makes psychological and "psychic" routines believable. If you've got a gift for improvization and are good at flattery, chances are you'll make a good mind-reader!

THE CENTRE TEAR

A mind-reader's dream: a spectator thinks of the name of someone important to them – it could be her boyfriend or a relative or a close friend – and writes it down on a slip of paper. The paper is folded up and burned, but as you look into the ashes you're able to reveal the name of the person she's thinking of.

This trick is totally impromptu. All you need is a slip of paper, about three inches square, a pen, a lighter and an audience. Have the lighter in your right pocket. Pick out a willing volunteer and tell her that you'd like to try an experiment. Ask her to think of the name of someone who means a lot to her: someone you couldn't possibly know, for instance her best friend. Take the paper, and in the centre draw a circle **(1)**.

Hand it to her along with the pen, saying, "I want you to write their name clearly in the middle of that circle and, as you write it, really try to bring that person to mind: how they looked, where you met them, any details that really bring them into sharp focus. Okay? And I don't want anyone else to look while she's doing this. Try to play along: I think you might find it interesting."

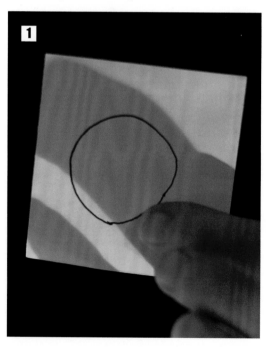

Turn your back on the girl as she writes the name on the paper. When she's finished, tell her to fold the paper in two so that the name is on the inside, and then fold it again so that it's in quarters. As she's doing this, get hold of an ashtray. Ask the girl if she's finished folding the paper and when she has, turn around to face her and take the paper from her as you say, "Just stand a bit closer to me." You tear the paper up as you say, "Do you still know this person or are they just a memory?"

As you do so, you're actually stealing away the circled centre of the paper which contains the name. Here's how: hold it with the corner which is actually the centre of the paper to the upper right and then tear it vertically down the middle **(2)**. The photos show your point of view.

Place the left-hand piece in front of the right-hand piece; in other words, furthest away from you. Rotate the two pieces 90 degrees in a clockwise direction and then tear again through the centre before again placing the left-hand pieces in front of the right-hand ones **(3)**.

Do the tearing as you're talking and keeping eye contact with the volunteer. Make it look like an unimportant exercise to which you're not really paying any attention. In fact, the top piece of paper, the one nearest you, is formed from the centre of the paper. It contains the name, completely untorn and ready to be read. You just have to sneak

it away from the other pieces to do that. That bit's easy.

Take all the pieces in the left hand but, as you do, pull back on the top piece with your right thumb. The thumb keeps this vital piece hidden behind the right fingers as the left hand drops the other pieces into the ashtray. At the same time you respond to the spectator's answer about whether she still knows the person whose name she's written down. "Good: I think this might work, then. There's just one more thing we have to do…"

With your right hand, reach into your pocket for the lighter and leave the folded piece of paper there as you take the lighter out. Use it to set the pieces of paper in the ashtray alight. Tell the girl to focus on the name of the person as the paper burns. "Stare into the flames and try to see an image: try to picture that person again."

But how do you read that piece of paper in your pocket? Well, there are all kinds of ways and which one you use very much depends on the situation in which you find yourself. If you have the girl next to you and the audience in front, then simply step behind her, slightly to her left, as she looks into the flames.

You can now put the lighter back in your pocket and palm the piece of paper out. Under cover of her body, you can flip open the piece of paper using your right hand and snatch a glimpse of it **(4)**.

You'll find that you can slip your thumb into the folded paper and, by pushing inwards, flip it open like an umbrella. Take your time. Open it slowly and quietly. Another way is to simply admit defeat. Amazingly, people are even more apt to believe that you can read minds if you occasionally tell them that the circumstances aren't quite right. They're so interested in seeing it work that they'll gladly give you a second chance. Tell the girl that nothing is coming through; she'll have to try again.

Give her another slip of paper and ask her to write the name down and fold the paper up, the same as before. Again you turn away from her, but this time you palm out the piece of paper from your pocket. As she's writing the name down again you've got all

the time in the world to read the name on the original palmed paper. Also, this time you can tell her to fold the paper and then tear it up herself. She puts it in the ashtray. You reach into your pocket for the lighter and dump the palmed piece. Then you set fire to the pieces of paper. This time, of course, when she gazes into the flames you're able to miraculously reveal the name.

Don't just reveal it in one fell swoop, though; stretch it out as if you're getting an impression of the name letter by letter. Don't call the letters out in order, either. Just say one or two of them before revealing the whole name: this allows the rest of the spectators to play along and try to guess it themselves. "I think there's an A in the name. An F… no, it's an R. And an M. An M at the beginning. And an I in the middle. M, A, R, I. Got it – it's Marilyn: is that right?"

If the spectators do manage to guess before you reveal the full name – and they will if you give them enough clues – they'll sometimes credit themselves with psychic powers too!

NOTES

This is the crux of a great mind-reading trick. You can frame lots of storylines around it. People can write anything down and you can always secretly read their thought. Sometimes I have the lighter in my inside left jacket pocket, but during the trick I go to my right-side pocket to get it. I fumble around as if I can't find it. This gives me time to open the slip in my pocket: then I "remember" where my lighter is. I bring my right hand out, the open paper hidden in my palm, and look at it as the hand moves across in front of me and into the inside jacket pocket. I leave the paper there as I take the lighter out. I've now got the info.

If you're at a table, open the slip on your lap and take a peek at it while covering your eyes with your hand in classic concentration pose. My favourite method is with just one person: I just ask them to close their eyes and think of the name, and when their eyes are closed I flip open the palmed paper and read. Cheeky but effective!

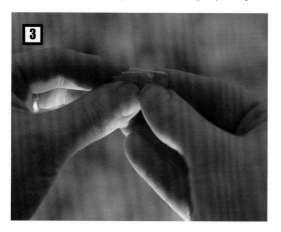

3

4

THE HAUNTED KEY

This little miracle makes it look as if you have the ability to move objects with the power of your mind. Just by concentrating, you make an ordinary key slowly revolve on your outstretched hand. And the best thing about it is that it's really easy to do.

You'll need an ordinary mortice key that's slightly longer than the width of your palm. The part that goes into the lock is known as the "bit". At the other end of the key is the "handle", a simple oval with a hole through the middle – this needs to be wide and heavy in relation to the bit. Lay the key across your open palm so that the bit is on your hand pointing towards you. The handle extends over the edge of the palm **(1)**.

"This key was given to me by my grandfather. He told me it was the key to a haunted house. I believed him, but then I was only six at the time. I don't really think it's the key to a haunted house. I don't even believe in haunted houses. But that doesn't mean there isn't something a little strange about it. Look..."

Hold your hand out so that everyone can see the key clearly. "Focus your mind on that key. Just for a second, imagine that it really does belong to a haunted house. Watch." Now slowly tip your hand ever so slightly so that the fingers dip imperceptibly towards the floor. If you have the right key, it will be so finely balanced that even the slightest tipping movement will cause it to revolve on your palm **(2)**.

Take it slow and easy: you don't want anyone to spot that you're tipping your hand. And keep up your storyline to build the spooky atmosphere.

"That's it, look: slowly the key moves by itself, as if turned by an invisible hand..." Once the key has started to revolve, it'll continue until it's rotated 180 degrees and it'll tend to speed up once it's past the half-way point. You can slow it down by tipping your hand back slightly the other way. "That's it – done."

And you know what the really weird thing is? When you get home, you'll find your back door unlocked. And if my grandfather's ghost has been around, your television will probably have gone too!"

NOTES

You can apparently prove to the audience that you're not moving your hand. Simply ask someone to hold your fingertips **(3)**. It makes no difference. Just raise the wrist instead of dipping the fingers to make the key turn. And take your time – the slower the key turns, the spookier it looks.

HEART-STOPPER

In this scary routine the dead seem to make themselves known, and you appear to temporarily become one of them! Half a dozen folded slips of paper have the names of people who are alive written on them, but one paper has the name of a person who's dead. They're mixed up, and yet you're able to divine the name of the dead person by a very strange method – when you touch that particular piece of paper, your pulse stops!

There are two different elements to this trick. The first is the method for making the pulse in your wrist stop. All you need to do is hide a golf ball or similar-sized object under your left armpit. Take the pulse in your left wrist; if you're normal and healthy it will beat away with a regular rhythm. When you want to stop your pulse, just gently squeeze your arm against the golf ball. The flow of blood to the wrist will stop and you might be surprised to find that your pulse just fades away to an apparent standstill **(1)**.

The photo shows an exposed view of the ball – you'd normally wear a jacket or have the ball inside your shirt. Obviously you don't want to be walking around all day clenching a golf ball under your armpit, so put it in a small bag and then safety-pin it to the inside of your jacket sleeve, or tape it to your shirt. That way, it's ready whenever you decide to perform the routine.

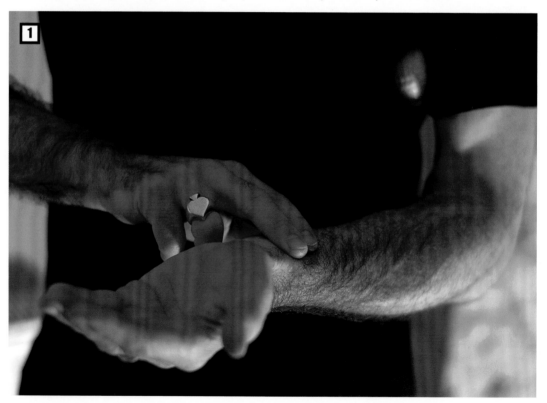

The second element of the trick is how you know which slip of paper has the dead name written on it. The answer lies in the pieces of paper: one of them is marked so that you can pick it out from the rest. There are lots of ways of marking the paper, but this is a particularly clever one. It uses a small, wire-bound notepad.

Take a craft knife and make clean slits at the top of the first page, between the punched holes that the binding goes through and the top edge of the paper. When you tear this page out it will look very different from the others because of the straight cuts. The holes in other pages torn from the book will be more uneven and ragged: see the difference in the photo. Here the holes with slits are to the left and right, with torn ones in the middle for comparison **(2)**.

If you don't want to use paper, try using postcards or the blank sides of business cards. Mark one of the cards on its edge by running the tip of a pencil along it. The markings can only be read if you tip the card edge-on towards you. Mark it on both long edges so that you can always read it without having to turn the card around.

Now you understand the basic principles, let me describe the routine in more detail because, as always, it's the way you present the trick that's going to make it effective. Take out the pad and some pens and say, "They say dead men tell no tales, but that's not true – let me show you." Tear out some pages from the notepad – six is plenty – and hand one to each of six spectators.

Be sure that you know who receives the marked paper. "I'd like you to think of someone close to you, but someone I couldn't know. And then I'll turn my back and I want you to write the name of that person on the piece of paper. Let me know when you've finished."

The spectators are ready to begin their task but you stop them, saying, "Oh, and one more thing – I want everyone to write the name of someone who's still alive today... everyone except you!" Point to the person who has the marked paper, saying, "I want you to write down the name of someone who's dead." There's a macabre tone to the request.

Turn your back while the spectators write down names. When they've finished, tell them to fold the papers in half and then ask someone to gather them and mix them up so that no one knows which one is which. You can now turn around again. This is when you ask for a volunteer to take your pulse; if you're wearing the ball under your left arm, then have them stand on your left side. Extend your left arm, bending it at the elbow, and ask them to take your pulse. If they're doing it properly you'll have your left hand palm-up and they'll have their fingers on your wrist – they should use their fingers, not the thumb. After a few moments they should be able to detect your steady pulse. "How am I?" you ask, jokingly. With any luck, they'll say that you seem just fine.

Ask someone to give you one of the slips of paper. Take it in your right hand and hold it to your forehead: but as you do so, get a glimpse of the torn edge of the paper. You're looking for those tell-tale straight cuts – if you don't see them, concentrate for a little while purely for effect and then ask the spectator for a report on your pulse. Of course, it's still normal. Hold the paper out, crush it into a ball and drop it to the floor. "Let me know if you feel anything different," you say to the spectator who's holding your wrist.

One at a time you take the slips of paper and hold them to your forehead before asking for a report on your well-being. When you see that you've got the marked slip in your hand, squeeze your arm slowly against the hidden ball. Your pulse will gradually fade away before coming to a stop. This won't escape the notice of the spectator holding your wrist. You don't need to say anything: the expression on their face will say it all. Pause, then take a deep breath and silently hand the slip to someone nearby.

At the same time, relax your left arm. Your pulse returns the moment the slip is put down; let your assisting spectator confirm this, then pick up the slip again. Your pulse disappears once more. The spectator will find this deeply disturbing. Look at the slip of paper and ask, "Who wrote the dead person's name?" Let that person identify themselves. Using both hands, open the paper towards you and read the name to yourself, then ask them to tell everyone the name. As they do, you dramatically turn the paper so that everyone can see you are holding the dead person's name in your hands. Hand the slip back to them, saying, "If I were you, I wouldn't hold on to it for too long!"

NOTES

You can use the business of stopping your pulse in a variety of ways. For instance, you could use it in combination with the Haunted Key; as the key rotates on one hand a spectator feels the pulse in your other wrist slowly come to a deathly stop. Or have someone write down the name of a dead person during the Centre Tear routine: the pulse in your wrist stops as you divine the name. The tricks in this book have been chosen to give you material which can be changed, altered and varied to suit your personal style and taste. Part of the joy of magic is creating routines which are your own. It's your chance to perform things no one has seen before. Make the most of that opportunity.

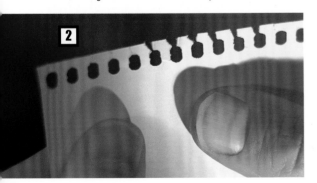

AHEAD OF THE GAME

In this baffling routine you appear to foretell the future. You predict in advance a date, a name and a playing card which each of three spectators will select. And you're 100 per cent accurate each time.

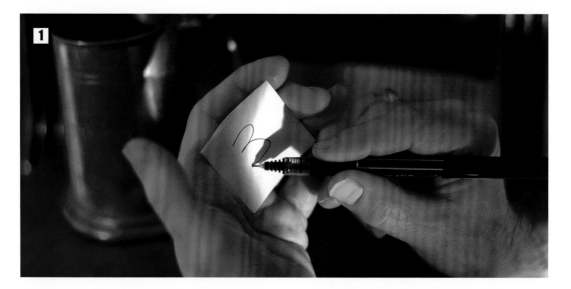

This routine uses what's known as the "one-ahead principle" although, as you'll see, it should really be named the "one-behind principle". It's been the building block of many a good mind-reading routine and you'll soon be using it to create your own.

For now, though, just follow the routine as described so that you can understand the workings. The theme is fortune-telling and you have some coins, a deck of playing cards, a pad of paper and a pen. You also need a cup or mug or even a baseball cap – any kind of receptacle into which you can place the three predictions.

Shuffle the deck of cards and then place it face-down nearby but, as you do so, catch a glimpse of the bottom card. Let's assume it's the three of clubs. Make sure that no one else sees this card.

Start the routine as a conversation about fortune-telling. Ask the spectators if they've ever had their fortune told. "Someone might have drawn up an astrological chart, read your palm, or maybe you broke open a fortune cookie and whatever it said inside freaked you out a bit. I don't believe that it's actually possible to tell the future,

but let me show you an interesting little experiment."

You're going to use three people for this trick. Let's assume that Bob is the first. Look him over as if trying to figure something out about his future and then write "Three of clubs" on the top sheet of the pad. Don't let anyone see the writing. Tear the sheet off and fold it into quarters with the writing inside. On the outside of the folded paper write the number 3 **(1)**. Don't tell anyone what you're doing, just do it and then drop the paper into the cup or hat, making sure that no one can see the number you wrote.

Now ask Bob to think of a month of the year. It can be the month of his birthday, his wedding anniversary, graduation or anything else. All you ask is that the month has some significance to him. "Which month did you choose?" He tells you and you ask him why he chose that particular month. Let's assume he chose May because that's when his birthday is. Frankly it doesn't matter to you at all, but it gives you a reason for him to tell you the month he's thinking of without arousing his suspicions. Move on to the second spectator, Susie. Ask her to think of a name: nothing too obscure. It should be the name of someone she knows, but not the name of anyone present. "And no pets," you say, as if anticipating her thoughts.

Look into her eyes. Then write something on the pad. Everyone there thinks that you're writing a name. In fact you're writing the month of "May" that Bob thought of. Make sure no one sees your writing or you'll be busted before you start. Tear off the sheet, fold it into quarters as before and write "1" on the side.

Drop the paper into the cup along with the first folded paper. You can now ask Susie to reveal the name of the person she was thinking of. Let's assume she tells you that she was thinking of Jake, the name of her ex-boyfriend. Make the relationship seem important: It'll disguise the fact that you're merely interested in finding out the name. As an aside, ask if she knows someone called John. You'll see why later.

Turn to the third spectator. "Steve, I want to try something different with you; not a month or a name or anything else that might already be in your mind. Let's pick something by chance instead." Pick up the pad, look at Steve and then write "John or Jake" on the top sheet. Tear the sheet off, fold it into quarters and then, again out of view, write a "2" on the side before dropping it into the cup. Now ask Steve to cut the deck of playing cards into two heaps. Take what was the lower portion of the deck and put it cross-ways on top of the other portion **(2)**. As you do this, you say, "Let's just mark the cut." Later you'll see how this manoeuvre, known as the cross-cut force, is used to force the original bottom card of the deck, the three of clubs, on to Steve.

"Okay," you say, "three predictions, three people. Let's see how we've done." Tip the three folded slips from the cup on to the table. Put slip number 1 in front of Bob, slip number 2 in front of Susie and slip number 3 in front of Steve. This is the first time the spectators see the numbers you wrote on the sides of the slips. "Bob, I asked you to choose a month. You chose the month of your birthday. When is that again?" He tells you that it's May. You open the slip of paper in front of him to reveal that May was the month you predicted. "Susie, I asked you to think of someone close. You thought of your ex. What was his name?" She reminds everyone that it was Jake. You open the slip of paper and she sees that you wrote down the names Jake and John. The extra name makes it look like you weren't quite sure. It's a convincing touch, since the name Jake is clearly there all the same. And it's not that dissimilar to John. It has to be more than coincidence.

"Steve, I didn't ask you to think of anything; I said that we'd let chance take a hand. Let's look at the card you cut to." You reach over and lift up the top half of the deck and turn it over **(3)**. It's the three of clubs. In actual fact the three of clubs was the original bottom card of the deck, but so much has happened since the cut was made that no one remembers which packet was where.

Ask Steve to open the slip of paper in front of him and read out your prediction. It says "Three of clubs". You've successfully predicted the future three times in a row. Expect a lot of invitations to the racetrack. ☞

NOTES

You can dress this trick in lots of different ways. There's no restriction on the kind of things people can think of: names, colours, numbers, places, animals etc. However, you'll always have to force one of the items, in this case the chosen playing card.

If you don't want to use playing cards you could use the dice force explained in the trick On a Roll in the Auto-Magic chapter. You know that if someone throws a pair of dice and adds the top and bottom numbers they'll always total 14. That's what you write on the first slip of paper. When you get to the third spectator, you ask him to roll the dice and do the addition to arrive at that figure.

I've got another more light-hearted approach to this trick in which no force is used; I employ a bit of humour instead. On the first slip of paper you write the date. By that, I mean that you write down today's date. When you get to the third spectator you ask him to take out a coin from his pocket and hold it tightly in his hand. He should make sure that no one knows what kind of coin he's got. Ask him to hold his closed hand up high as you stare at it. You say, "Now, it would be impossible for me to tell you which coin you've got: it's hidden in your hand and no one can see it." Then you write something on your pad. You're working the one-ahead principle as usual and writing down whatever it was that the second spectator chose. Fold the slip, write the number 2 on its side and drop it into the cup.

Keep him there holding the coin up in his closed hand. At the finish of the trick, reveal that you got predictions 1 and 2 correct. Everyone should be suitably impressed. Now look at the third spectator. "You were the most difficult. You were the most sceptical. And I wonder if you'd really be impressed if I just told you what coin you're holding in your hand – maybe that's not enough. But what if I could tell you the date? That would be impressive, right?" He'll agree, thinking that you mean the date on the coin. "Okay, then: take a look."

He goes to take a look at the coin but what you really meant was to take a look at the paper, because you now open the third slip and show it to the spectators, saying, "I said I'd tell you the date. And this is it. The fourth of July!" Sure enough, written across the paper is today's date, whatever it happens to be. That should get a laugh. Finish by complimenting the third spectator, "I know a sceptic when I see one, and I know to quit while I'm ahead – two out of three ain't bad!"

This is a much less serious approach to the routine but it can be more suitable if you're at a party or bar or in some situation where you just want to have a laugh rather than selling them the idea that you're in touch with the dark side, or, indeed, when you don't have cards or dice to hand to use for the force.

The routine works really well on special occasions such as Halloween, Easter, Christmas or New Year, in which case I modify the last line: "That's the date, December 31, and so I'll take this opportunity to wish you a very happy New Year!" It makes a nice, fun sign-off to the routine.

MAGIC SQUARE

A magic square is a mathematical arrangement of 16 numbers in a 4 x 4 grid. The amazing thing is that all the rows and columns in the grid add up to exactly the same number. So do the diagonals and even the corners. It would take a genius to construct one of these mathematical oddities for a number the spectator picks at random, and yet that's exactly what you do. They choose a number and you instantly create a magic square: you genius, you!

The magic square in the illustration adds up to the number 36 **(1)**. Take a good look at it: each vertical and horizontal column of four numbers adds up to 36. So do the diagonals and the four corners. In fact, if you take the centre block of four numbers, they also add up to 36. You can find similar blocks all over the square and they all add up to 36. Amazing isn't it? And yet you can learn to do this quite easily. Here's how.

There's a trick to constructing the square that the audience aren't aware of – when you start this trick, you already know what 12 of the 16 numbers will be even though you have no idea what number the spectator will choose. These numbers are always the same; all you have to do during the performance is use a secret mathematical formula to work out what the remaining four numbers will be. ☞

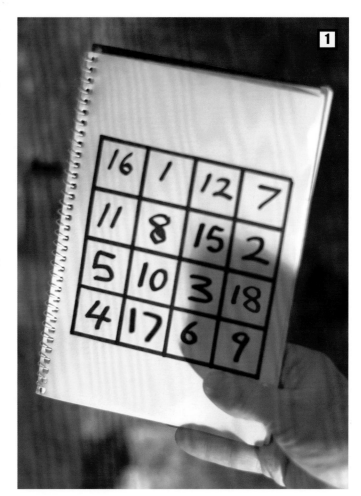

Let's take the top left cell as an example. It needs to be filled with R + 1. That's 28 + 1 which is 29. So you'd write 29 in that cell. Make the same kind of calculation with the other four empty cells and write the results in there. At the end you'll have filled in all four empty cells and completed the square **(3)**.

All the horizontal and vertical rows in this magic square add up to the chosen number. So do all the four corners and the diagonals and any other block of four numbers you choose.

You can see that the mechanics of the trick are easier that you'd expect, but you might be worried about remembering the 12 original numbers. I used to carry a little piece of card in my wallet with the template for the magic square drawn on it. When I wanted to do the trick I'd use it as a reference and secretly copy a bigger version of it down on to a sheet of paper, the back of an envelope or a napkin, and I made sure that the paper was nearby when I started the trick, which I did by turning to a girl I wanted to impress, saying, "Do you know what your lucky number is?" Okay, not the greatest chat-up line in the world, but enough to get into the routine.

No matter what her response was, I'd follow up by saying something along the lines of, "There's an interesting way of working out your lucky number: let's try something. Just clear your mind and then give me a number between, say, 30 and 100." She'd call out a number and I'd tell her, "Now that is lucky. You couldn't have picked a better number. Does it mean anything special to you or did you just pick it at random?"

Make as much as you can out of her response. You want her to feel there was something special about the way she chose that number. Then I'd pick up a pen and take out the envelope or napkin (facing towards me, so she didn't see my earlier scribbling) saying, "I

The numbers in red are the ones you have to calculate during the performance **(2)**. It works like this: You ask someone to call out a number between, say, 30 and 100. Let's assume they choose 49. No matter what number they choose, you mentally subtract 21 from it. In this instance 49 − 21 equals a Remainder of 28.

Remember this Remainder, because you'll now use it to calculate the four missing numbers. Photo 2 shows you what you need to do in each case. The red letter R represents the Remainder.

haven't done this for a long time; let me see if I can still do it. I want you to time me." Ask her to look at her watch, and when the second hand reaches 12 she's to say, "Go." When 60 seconds have passed, she's to say "Stop." Repeat the number she chose so she and anyone else watching will remember it. As soon as she says "Go," start writing as fast as you can.

You pretend to draw the lines that make up the square you've already drawn (and since you're supposedly doing this at speed, make sure that the square looks like it's been drawn in a hurry in the first place). Then you pretend to fill in numbers.

Of course, the only thing you really have to do is calculate the four missing numbers and insert those. Make it look as if you really are pushed for time on this one. As soon as the girl shouts "Stop," put the paper down. "Nearly didn't make it," you say. "Let's see if I got it right." Ask the girl to choose one of the vertical columns of numbers. "Don't think about it. Just pick any of the four columns." When she's made a choice, you slowly and openly add those numbers up. She should be amazed when they add up to her chosen number. Add them up again as if to make sure. Write the number down next to the magic square. "Now, that was lucky," you say. "Let's try another column. Choose another."

She does, and together you add those numbers up. Again, they add up to her "lucky" number. Smile, and then point out that all the vertical columns add up to her number. Give her time to check that this is actually true. Then put the paper down. Pause for a moment and then pick the magic square up again as if you've just noticed something. "I don't believe this: choose a horizontal row of numbers." She does – and they too add up to her lucky number. In fact, all of the rows add up to the number she chose. Then point out that the diagonals' four numbers also add up to the same number. "And finally – and I've never had this happen before – if you total up the four corner numbers, they also add up to your lucky number!"

Hand her the magic square. Believe me, she'll want to keep this. It makes a great souvenir. And if you're lucky, she might ask for your number too!

NOTES

This trick can be worked anywhere; you can do it one-on-one as a small demonstration of your mental prowess or as a big feature trick in a more formal show. If you use it regularly, I'd recommend that you memorize the square. Don't be frightened of this; it's just twelve numbers and no more difficult than remembering two of your friends' phone numbers.

The formula for the empty cells is easy to remember, too: there are only four cells to fill and you either do nothing, add 1, add 2 or add 3 – how hard can that be? All right, then; if you're that lazy, just write a crib note on your wrist!

Chapter eight
STREET SCAMS

Magic and scams have always been intertwined. In the Middle Ages, while the street magician was performing his tricks, his accomplice would be robbing the crowd. These days magicians often use their knowledge to reveal how scam artists operate – many have advised law enforcement agencies and casinos. Being experts in trickery, manipulation and psychology, there's no better person to turn to if you think a scam is in operation. In this chapter you'll learn some classic street tricks – for entertainment only, obviously!

THREE-CARD MONTE

This is the world's most famous street scam, the Three-Card Monte, aka Find the Lady. You show three cards, two similar, one different, often a Queen. Keep your eye on the Queen. You mix up the face-down cards and ask someone to find the lady. They fail.

So you do it again. And again they fail. This time they can't miss: you've bent the corner of the Queen, making it easy to spot. Guess what? They miss again. It's a 100 per cent con trick and they've just been suckered by a master hustler – you!

The history of the Three-Card Monte goes back to the 18th century and you'll still find it played all over the world today. Sometimes the conmen use playing cards, sometimes they use plastic, rubber or leather discs with a piece of paper stuck to one of them. The idea that it's a fair game of chance is just a way of hooking you; the outcome is always the same – you lose.

Even when you've learned how it works, don't be tempted to play for real – it's a game run by hardcore gangs whose sole purpose is to take you for whatever cash you have. They have no scruples and more often than not there are more players involved than you might at first realize; in addition to the operator there'll usually be a stooge or two in the crowd as well as lookouts and heavies. Don't ever challenge them. Trust me: you *will* lose.

The Props

The routine here employs the same basic moves the conmen use. You'll need three cards. Two are identical: say, the nine of hearts. The third is a contrasting card, for example the Queen of spades. Prepare the cards by placing them together and then bending them in the middle along their length. This bend makes the cards easier to pick up by the ends. One further bit of preparation is to weaken the outer right and inner left corners of the cards. Just bend them backwards and forwards a few times, but don't break them; you'll learn why shortly. Now let's start at the beginning.

Throwing the Cards

Lay the three cards face-down with the Queen in the middle **(1)**. Pick up the outer two cards, one in each hand. The thumb holds the inner end of the card while the middle finger holds the outer end of the card **(2)**. ☞

151

Now pick up the Queen too, so it's below the card already held in the right hand **(3)**. The thumb is at the inner end of the Queen but the outer end is held by the third finger rather than the middle one.

This grip makes it easy for you to throw the Queen down without dropping the other card in your hand. "Three cards: one's a Queen. Keep your eye on the Queen 'cos this is a game of Find the Lady." Turn your hands palm-up to display the cards. Then turn them palm-down again, holding them about nine inches above your work surface.

You now throw all three cards back down, one at a time, as you say, "One, two, three cards." Move your right hand to the left and throw the Queen, face-downwards **(4)**. Move your right hand back and then toss the left-hand card across in the other direction so that it lands to the right of the Queen, leaving a space between them **(5)**.

Finally, toss the remaining right-hand card down, in the space you just left, so that it becomes the middle card of the row. You should throw the cards so that the spectators can't see their faces as they're going down **(6)**. "Okay, where's the Queen?" you ask.

If the spectators have been watching properly, they'll point to the card on your left. Turn it over and show them that they're correct. "Well done." But the conman has already suckered you in on the first stage of the Monte hustle. He's got you playing along and you actually think this is a game that you might be able to win. Let me show you why you can't. "Let's start again." Turn the Queen face-down and put it back in the middle of the row. "The Queen's in the middle again. Watch her go." ☞

The Fake Throw

You appear to repeat the same handling again but in fact this is where you work a switch, and instead of throwing the Queen to the left of the row, you'll have it end up in the middle.

Pick up the cards exactly as before. The Queen is the lower card of the two in the right hand. Turn the hands over and show the Queen once again. Then turn the hands palm-down. The right hand appears to toss the Queen to the left as before, but actually you keep hold of it, release your grip with the middle finger and let go of the upper card instead **(7)**. You need to practice to make sure that this fake throw looks exactly like the real throw, but it's not as difficult as you'd imagine. Just make the move at the same pace as the genuine throw. So instead of the Queen going to the left, a nine of hearts is tossed down instead. The left hand now throws its card to the right, leaving a gap between it and the first card.

Finally, the right hand throws its remaining card into the space between the two face-down cards. This puts the Queen in the middle. "Business as usual. Where's the lady?" Everyone should point to the card on your left again. Turn it over to show that they're wrong. Turn over the right-hand nine and then the middle card to reveal it's the Queen. "Don't worry about not getting it right. Very few people do. I'll show you why."

The Convincer

You appear to repeat the last phase again but this time you add an extra bit of business which will convince people even more that the Queen must be on the left.

"Let's start again." All the cards are once again face-down with the Queen in the middle. Pick the cards up exactly as before and turn your hands over to show the Queen on the bottom of the right-hand cards again. Make the same throwing moves as described in the Fake Throw. This positions the Queen in the middle.

As soon as the cards have landed, follow up with this sequence of moves: The right hand picks up the middle card between the thumb and middle finger. Without showing the face, it then picks up the card on the right below it. This card is held between the thumb and third finger. It's the same starting position for the fake throw, except that the Queen is above the nine this time. Turn your right hand palm-up as you say, "No lady here." This displays the nine.

Use the fake throw to apparently toss it immediately to the right of the card already on the table. The fake throw means it's actually the Queen which goes down instead. Now turn your right hand palm-up again, showing the same nine. "And no lady here." Throw this card face-down to the right of the two cards already down. Point to the card on your left: "So you know that she must be here... don't

you?" Wait a beat and then flip the card face-up. The audience will be shocked to see that it's not the Queen. Flip the card on the right end of the row face-up to reveal another nine. Then flip the middle card over to show the Queen. "She's always in the middle."

The Bent Corner

This final phase makes use of the fact that you softened the corners of the cards earlier. "Sometimes the hustler has a secret accomplice, known as a shill, in the crowd. The hustler will glance away as though he'd been distracted by something and the shill will quickly lean forward, pick up the Queen and mark it by bending the corner like this." Hold all three cards in a fan with the Queen on top. You bend up the outer right corner of the Queen **(8)**.

Place it face-down with the bent corner towards the spectators. The right hand now comes over the other two cards and, as it takes the top one, the third finger secretly bends its corner up. This is easy; the left hand holds the cards and the third finger just pushes up on the softened corner of the top card **(9)**. The photo shows an exposed view. This card is held in your right hand in the usual position with the fingers hiding the bent corner. The left hand takes the other card in a similar position. The right hand moves over the Queen and picks it up as before in preparation for the false throw. "Remember: the Queen's got the bent corner." Turn both hands face-up momentarily to show the cards, then down again. Pretend to throw the Queen to the left, but actually use the fake throw to toss the other card instead. The left hand throws its card to the right, leaving the customary space between it and the card on the left. At the same time, your right hand moves towards you and the right third finger retains its grip on the outer end of the card as the little finger pushes down on the bent corner to straighten it.

The more you soften this corner before the trick, the easier ☞

it will be to straighten out. The right hand drops its card, the Queen, with the corner now straightened, into the middle of the row. "Anyone should be able to find the lady now," you say, pointing to the bent corner. "You know that she isn't here or here."

The right hand picks up the middle card and then the card on the right and then you again perform the convincer, apparently showing both the cards as nine of hearts. "But, as I said, don't bet on it. The only sure thing is that you'll lose." Turn the card on the left over. It's a nine. Then the card on the right. "You know what they say about a fool and his money..." Finally, turn over the Queen in the middle. "They were lucky to get together in the first place!"

NOTES

It's usually better to perform the Three-Card Monte as a demonstration rather than an actual gambling game unless you're incredibly good at it. Once they start to lose, or if you move the cards around too quickly, people will usually stop trying to follow the Queen and just guess where it is instead. And, by the law of averages, they'll sometimes be right!

Instead, it's safer to present the trick as a story about how con games work. That way, the spectators can enjoy it for the clever trick it is rather than feeling you're challenging them to a battle of wits.

FAST AND LOOSE

A really old con game using a loop of chain. You lay it on the table in a doubled-up figure-of-eight pattern. All the spectator has to do is put his finger in one of the two loops, "One of those loops is lucky – if your finger traps the chain as I pull it away, you win. If the chain comes free, you lose. It's a fifty-fifty chance."

You demonstrate, trapping the chain around your own finger, and then lay down the pattern again. He chooses and puts his finger into one of the loops. And you, of course, pull the chain completely free of his finger. He can try again and again, but he'll never catch that loop. Why? Because it's a complete scam, that's why.

The Props

This game has been played for centuries and was even mentioned in Shakespeare's *King John*. It was played at racecourses and markets and often used to relieve sailors of their hard-earned bounty as they arrived back at port after long voyages, being played on top of upturned barrels on the dockside. One version was known as "Prick the Garter" and was played with a belt which was folded in half and then rolled up. Its simplicity makes it very beguiling, and yet it's completely impossible to win. All you need is a three- or four-foot length of chain fastened into a loop. The chain should be thin and not too heavy; ball-chain, as used for attaching plugs to baths or basins, works well.

The secret is that when you lay out the figure-of-eight shape on the table, you can make it so that the spectator has a fair chance at the game – one loop will indeed hold fast and the other will come loose from his finger. But if you lay it down in a slightly different fashion the spectator can never win, no matter which loop he chooses.

Holding Fast

Lay the chain on the table so that it forms a long loop. Place your right middle finger down into the right-hand end of the loop and lift it up **(1)**. "This is an old gambling game. All you have to do is try to trap this chain by sticking your finger inside one of two loops. Let me show you."

Sweep the end of the chain around in an anti-clockwise arc, turning the hand palm towards you, and then lay it on the table so that you're forming the pattern shown in the photo **(2)**. Stick your fingers and thumbs into the end loops of the pattern and then move them apart to open them up **(3)**. Then squeeze the top and bottom lengths of the chain together, creating a figure-of-eight or bowtie shape. "You can see that there are now two loops: one on the left and one on the right. And I'm going to pull the chain from here **(4)**.

Now, logically, if you put your finger inside one of these two it'll trap the chain because it's inside of it. But if you put your finger in the other one, it'll be on the outside of the chain's loop and so ☞

I'm able to pull it free. If you trap the chain, you win a prize. So which one do you want to choose? The left or the right?"

Let the spectator answer and then toy with him a little, saying, "Is that my left or yours?" Once he's decided, get him to put his forefinger into that loop. The situation here is that if you place your finger in the loop to your left **(5)**, when you pull the chain you'll see that it will catch "fast" **(6)**. But if you put your finger in the loop to your right and pull, the chain will come free **(7)**.

The spectator can choose and genuinely has a fair fifty-fifty chance

of winning. "Good; now, I'm going to pull the chain away and if it catches on your finger, you win. This is just a trial run, though." Pull the chain and comment on the result: he's either a winner or a loser. If the chain came free, commiserate with him and offer him another go. I keep letting him try it until he chooses the loop on my left and catches the chain. Then I say, "Okay, the prize you've won is that you get another go – but this time it's for real: get your money out!"

Coming Loose

This time you lay the chain on the table so that it doesn't matter which loop he chooses: the chain will always come free and he'll lose. This time you take hold of the chain by putting your finger underneath the back strand of chain at the right side and up into the loop – a subtle difference that won't be noticed **(8)**.

Again, sweep your hand around in an anti-clockwise direction, throwing the loop of chain on to the table. Widen the loops with your thumb and forefingers and then pull the outer strands together to form a figure-of-eight. Apart from the initial pick-up of the chain with the middle finger, these are exactly the same moves as before. "More difficult when it's for money, isn't it? Just kidding: this one's on the house. Pick a loop. If your finger catches the loop, you're a winner. If the chain comes free, the drinks are on you."

The spectator chooses a loop and you again take hold of the chain at the point nearest to you on the right. Regardless of which loop he put his finger in, when you pull the chain it will come away **(9)**. "Not your lucky day my friend." Let him lose a couple more times before moving on to the next phase.

Double Jeopardy

In this sequence, you give him two chances to win. "Look, I'll help you." Lay down the chain in the "no win" configuration again and then make him an offer he can't refuse. "Tell you what: stick a finger in each loop. It'll be easier if each finger's on a different hand!" He does as you ask. Pick up the chain at your right side again and pull so that it tightens against both of his fingers. "You

can feel that. It's going to catch against one of your fingers… but which one?" Keep hold of the chain, but slacken the tension. "I'll count to three and you take one of your fingers out."

Make the count and let him take a finger out of one of the loops. Pull the chain. It comes free. He made the wrong choice yet again!

Sucker Finish

You give him one last chance to win. You couldn't make it any easier for him. He can see you making that loop: the loop that will catch around his finger. And yet somehow, it just melts away when he tries to catch it.

Here's why. Start in exactly the same way as before, with your right middle finger under the chain and up through the loop of it. This time, though, as you sweep the chain around and throw it down, keep your finger in the loop on the tabletop. He should be absolutely convinced that your finger on the table marks the exact spot his finger should be if he wants to win this game. "Keep your eyes on that spot. Don't let me misdirect you. In fact, put your finger there now." **(10)**.

He does so, and you form the chain into the usual figure-of-eight even though his finger is on the table. "Now, this time you know for certain that your finger's inside the chain, same as mine was. You can't lose." Slowly pull on the chain. "Or can you?" To his surprise and dismay, once again it will come free.

NOTES

This is one of my favourite scams. Be sure to follow the instructions carefully. Once you understand how the different layouts are made, you should have no difficulty in working the mechanics of the trick.

The challenge then is to do it with a smile and get away with it. Remember, no one likes to be a loser, particularly when they're playing your game with your rules, so try as much as possible to deflect any confrontation with humour; the goal, as always, is to entertain your audience and have a bit of fun *with* them, rather than at their expense. 🖐

THE SHELL GAME

This gambling scam has made suckers of thousands of people. The hustler covers a small pea with half a walnut shell and then mixes it up with two other shells. Can you find the one which has the pea underneath? Of course you can't! As with the Three-Card Monte, variations of this game are played all over the world using anything from matchbox drawers to bottle caps and thimbles – I even saw a gang in Barcelona using hollowed-out slices of carrot!

The Props

For this version you'll need three half-walnut shells which are as identical as possible, a small rubber pea and a soft surface to work on **(1)**. You can carve the pea out of a bit of rubber or sponge, or you can buy specially-made peas and shells for this trick from magic suppliers. A tablecloth or folded newspaper makes an ideal work-surface: alternatively, you can use your jacket draped over a table or bar stool.

The secret of the Shell Game is that if you cover the pea with the shell and push it forward, the pea will become trapped by the rear edge of the shell which rides over it, causing it to pop out from under the back. You'll have to experiment to get the right feel for the trick. Press down lightly and push forwards: when you're applying just the right amount of pressure, the pea will appear from underneath the back edge of the shell almost automatically.

The Steal

"This is the simplest game in the world. It uses three little shells and a pea. All you have to do is keep your eye on the pea." Place the pea down near you and cover it with one of the shells. Position the other two either side of it. "This is the easy bit: where's the pea at the moment?" You hope the spectators will point to the middle shell. "Good: I can see that university education paid off!" Move the centre shell forward with your left hand; the pea pops out from under the back of the shell and you grip it between your fingers **(2, 3, 4)**.

Once it's secure, let go of the shell and, without changing the position of the fingers, use the same hand to push the other two shells forward so that all three are in line again a couple of inches further forward than the original row. The pea remains gripped between the fingers of the left hand: not for long, though. ☞

The Load

Place your left hand on the left shell and your right hand on the right shell. They adopt the same position as you used for the steal: forefingers on top, thumb behind. Swap the positions of the outer two shells, sliding them along the tablecloth without lifting them up. To the spectator, you've simply swapped the outer shells. Since he still believes the pea to be under the centre shell, this move is of no consequence. Briefly take your hands off the shells **(5)**.

The left hand, hiding the pea, returns to your left side, the right hand to your right. Now drag the two outer shells back in line with the centre one. However, as you pull back the left-hand shell, you load the pea underneath it. This is very easy. Just let the pea contact the surface of the table and drag the shell back over the top of it. It's the exact reverse of the steal and it happens invisibly and almost automatically. "Okay, now: where's the pea?"

The spectator has no reason to think that it's anywhere but underneath the middle shell. Lift up the centre shell to show that the pea isn't there. "Unlucky. It's not easy, though!" Replace the shell, then lift the one on the right to reveal the pea.

The Routine

By using the Steal and the Load you can make the pea disappear from any shell and then reveal it under another. It's best not to overdo this or people might catch on: remember less is more with many tricks. I usually follow up the opening moves by putting the pea back on the table and covering it with the left-hand shell. Push all the shells forward and steal the pea again in the process. Use both hands to swap round the two outer shells. Anyone following will think that the pea is now under the right-hand shell.

"This time I'll give you a two-to-one chance: which one do you think the pea *isn't* under?" Generally they'll point to the middle shell. But it doesn't matter which shell they point to because the pea is actually still hidden between your left fingers. When they point to a shell, drag it backwards out of the line, saying, "Not that one, then? Okay." At the same time you secretly load the pea under it. Ask them to turn their chosen shells over one at a time. They're both empty. Lift the remaining shell to reveal the pea. "Bad luck, buddy!"

At this stage I place the shell back over the pea and push it forward so that it's back in line with the other two, stealing it out again in the process. Then I reach for my wallet, at the same time ditching the pea in my pocket. I take some cash out and put it on the table, saying, "Okay, one last chance: this time we'll only use two shells." I move all three shells around and then turn one of them over to show it empty. "Just two shells on the table along with my cash. Any takers?" You're only joking, but you can keep the audience in suspense for a while saying, "Really: I'm only turning the next shell over if there's someone else's money on the table besides mine! No takers? Don't blame you" – I put the wallet away

again – "because this is one of the oldest scams in the world. And it's a scam you ain't never gonna win. Have a look."

Gesture for the spectators to lift the shells. When they do, they find that the pea has disappeared.

Glass Finale

For an added convincing touch you need a shot glass. Put the pea under the centre shell and then place the glass upside-down over it **(6)**. Push the glass and shell forward. Amazingly, the pea will slip out from under both the shell and the glass and once again end up gripped between your fingers.

Ask someone to put their finger on top of the glass. "Don't move. Don't let anyone in or out." Drag one of the remaining shells towards you and load the pea under it. Ask someone else to put their finger on top of it. "And we don't need this one." Casually show the third shell empty as you put it in your pocket. "The game's part scam, part illusion. You think the pea's under here, but watch." Snap your fingers and then ask the person touching the glass to lift it up. They lift the shell and find that the pea's gone.

"If you want to know how it's done, ask him," you say, pointing to the other person. He lifts the shell he's holding and finds that the pea has somehow appeared underneath it.

NOTES

The Shell Game is a genuine scam, but it plays just as well as a trick as it does a hustle. Build a nice series of moves which flow, come up with some simple storyline that seems to explain it and then end with a surprise such as the pea vanishing altogether or the shot glass finish.

The way you grip the pea is unusual: you can't really call it a palm. When it's clipped between your fingers you might think that the position of your hand looks suspicious. It might if you held your hand that way in any other trick, but in this one it's perfectly natural to move the shells around by placing your fingers on top and your thumb behind: keep the hands in that position as much as possible during the routine and you shouldn't encounter any suspicion.

Chapter nine
PARTY TRICKS

There's no better audience than party-goers but the tricks have to play big so that the whole room can appreciate them. In this chapter I've described some of my favourites – killer routines designed to make your audience whoop with laughter or scream in surprise. Don't do them all at once though – always hold one trick back because if the party starts to die down you're sure to be asked to do one more piece of magic. That's when you hit them with your very best trick – the one that'll have you remembered long after the party's forgotten.

VOODOO ASH

Do you believe in voodoo? Your audience might after you've performed this eerie ritual. A girl holds her hand closed into a fist out in front of her. You dab some cigarette ash on to your own palm, "That's the black spot of doom," you say, cheerily. You rub it away until it's all but disappeared. But when she opens her hand, the black spot of doom has reappeared right in the middle of her palm.

This is one of the best tricks you'll ever do. It's got so many good things going for it: there's no set-up, you can do it almost anywhere and it always goes down well, especially if you dress it with some suitable storyline. Pick the right spectator and you're sure of a scream when she opens her hand. The only requirement is that there's an ashtray and some smokers present.

Tell them that you want to use some ash from their cigarettes, so for the moment they can smoke all they like; they'll see why in a moment. Now you begin your story. "Do you believe in voodoo?

A lot of people do. They believe that if a voodoo priest sticks a needle in a wax doll, the pain of that needle will transfer to the victim. How does it work? Is it black magic or is it all in the mind? I don't suppose it matters as long as it has the same effect. The only question is: does it work? Let's try some voodoo and see."

It's best to choose a girl to help with this one. They tend to react better than guys to this particular trick. If there's a girl smoking, choose her. "Can I borrow you for a moment? You won't need that cigarette." Take it away from her and stub it out in the ashtray.

As you do, dab the tip of your middle finger into the ashtray and secretly get some ash on it. We'll assume, as usual, that you're right-handed, so the ash is on your right middle finger. Ask the girl to stand opposite you. "Hold your hands out palm-down. Fingers straight, thumbs out. A bit higher." As you say, "A bit higher", you take hold of her hands and raise them a few inches. Your right middle finger presses gently against her left palm **(1)**. This transfers some of the ash, leaving a black mark on her palm. She won't feel this; she'll be concentrating on following your instructions.

Ask, "Are you right- or left-handed?" If she says "Right-handed", say rather pointedly, "Okay, we don't want to damage it, then; put it down, out of the way. Now close your other hand into a fist." You demonstrate with your left hand. If she says she's left-handed, you say, "Okay, let's use that hand, then. Put the other one down: now close your left hand into a fist." And again you demonstrate what you want done. "Voodoo priests use a special powder. They sprinkle it into their victim's food, or blow it into their face. It's supposed to turn you into a zombie." Pause here and stare into her eyes. "You see how the psychology works? I haven't even done that to you yet and you're already going into a trance!" Pick up the ashtray and openly dip your right middle finger into the ash. "Seeing as I haven't got any of that powder, let's make do with some ash instead."

Put the ashtray down and then use your finger to place a smudge of ash in the middle of your left palm **(2)**. ☞

"The other thing that the voodoo priest needs is something personal which belongs to the victim. A possession, or some strands of hair or nail clippings. They mould them into the wax of the doll. Now, this ash came from your cigarette: maybe that'll work instead." Hold your left hand out and show the black spot on your palm. "It looks innocent enough, but ash is a very powerful symbol: in many cultures it symbolizes death. A black spot of doom: watch..."

With your right hand, rub away the spot from your left palm and then brush your hands together to get rid of the last traces of ash. Everyone will be quite rightly wondering where all this is leading. Some might even be anticipating what happens next. Look at the girl who's still holding her fist closed. "There's only one way to get rid of a voodoo curse... and that's to transfer it to someone else. Let's see if it's worked. Open your hand."

Prepare for a squeal of surprise as she opens her hand and sees the ash in the middle of her palm **(3)**.

NOTES

One magician who created a sensation with this trick was Heba Haba Al of Chicago. He worked as a bar magician, and as he served customers and entertained them with tricks, he secretly put a spot of ash on all of their palms. Then, once a suitable length of time had elapsed, he'd perform the ash trick on someone; usually a pretty girl. Everyone was amazed when the ash appeared on the girl's hand. But they were absolutely stunned when he told them all to look at their own hands – every single person at the bar found a black spot right in the middle of their palm.

You don't need to use cigarette ash for this trick: a lipstick or eye shadow or similar cosmetic product will work equally well. All you need to do is carry some around with you and secretly get a smudge of it on your finger before you start the trick. Look for a girl who's wearing a similar shade to the one you've got and ask her to help. She takes her lipstick out and hands it to one of the other spectators. You secretly place a smudge of lipstick on her palm as originally described.

Only after this preparation is complete do you take her lipstick and open it. Comment on the colour as if you'd only just noticed it. If the colour of the lipstick is even vaguely red, refer to it as "blood" in your storyline.

You can draw a dot of colour on your palm, or do what I sometimes do and mark a dot in the centre of a piece of paper, or even some paper money if you're feeling rich. Mumble some made-up voodoo words as you set fire to the paper and watch it burn away in an ashtray. You can make this performance as dramatic or as funny as you like. Finally the girl opens her hand and is shocked to find that she's been marked with the voodoo spot of doom!

DOWN IN ONE

You suggest a party game. A glass is wrapped in a napkin so that no one can see inside it and then a coin is spun on the table. The glass is placed over the coin. Here's the game – they have to guess whether the coin will fall heads-up or tails-up. Actually, it really doesn't matter, because while the audience is considering that question, the glass completely disappears.

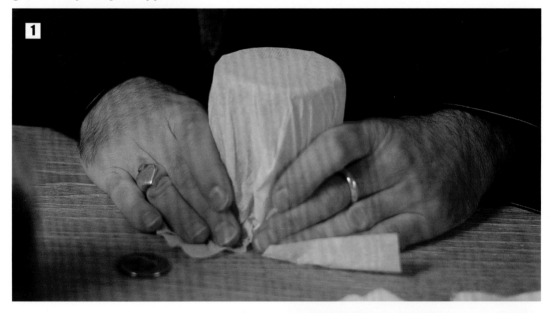

This trick is best performed at a table or bar. You need a whisky glass or other tumbler, a paper napkin and a coin. "Have you seen this?" you ask, taking out a coin and spinning it on the table. "A guy showed it to me in a bar." Pick up the empty tumbler and, if it's damp inside, wipe it out with a paper napkin, then cover it with a second one. Just mould the napkin around the shape of the glass **(1)**. Leave the edges splayed out. They mustn't be folded inside the mouth of the glass, for reasons which will become clear later.

You're seated at the table holding the covered glass in your left hand. Pick up the coin in your right hand and spin it on the table so that it twirls around in one spot. "It's a kind of game: the guy spun the coin, covered it and then asked everyone to guess whether the coin would land heads or tails up." Do exactly as you say, covering ☞

the spinning coin with the glass **(2)**. "What do you reckon – heads or tails?" When someone calls out "Heads" or "Tails" you lift the glass, bringing it towards you and near the edge of the table while keeping your eye fixed on the coin. If they're right, congratulate them. If they're wrong, commiserate. "That's all this guy was doing – except that he could guess it right every single time." Pick up the coin, give it another spin and cover it with the glass. "I don't know if it's something to do with the sound that the coin makes as it slows down. Heads or tails – what do you think this time?"

People make their guesses and you lift the glass once again to reveal whether they're right or wrong. This time you bring the glass towards you and beyond the edge of the table. Relax your grip on the napkin slightly and the glass will drop from under it on to your lap **(3)**. The photo shows an exposed view from the side.

Have your legs held up and together ready to catch it, otherwise there'll be some unnecessary misdirection created by it rolling off your lap and smashing on the floor! Although the glass has gone, if you hold the napkin gently it'll retain its shape. Move it back over the table and then spin the coin again. Cover the spinning coin with the glass-shaped napkin **(4)**. "But it wasn't just the coin trick that had me puzzled...it was this." Bring your right hand over the napkin, let it hover for a second and then slam it down hard **(5)**.

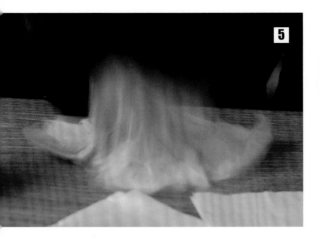

The glass-shaped napkin collapses under your hand – the glass has completely disappeared. This should come as a real shock to the spectators. Immediately reach under the table with your left hand to a position that's directly below your right hand and the crushed napkin but, as you do so, pick up the glass from your lap.

Turn the mouth of the glass against the underside of the table a couple of times to make a noise that sounds like you're struggling to pull it right through the wood. "He made the glass go right through the table – look." Bring the glass out from under the table, but don't bring it back over the edge that's nearest to you.

Instead, extend your arm to the left and bring it back over the left edge of the table. This little touch makes the trick more convincing:

it helps throw the audience off the idea that the glass somehow went around the side of the table nearest to you. Slam the glass down on top of the table to emphasize its solidity. Then lift the napkin. The coin is still there and the table is still solid. "I've no idea how he did it!"

NOTES

There's another way of reproducing the glass after it's disappeared which works if you're wearing a jacket. As soon as the glass has vanished, lift the napkin to reveal that only the coin remains beneath it. Crumple the napkin into a ball, throw it away and hand the borrowed coin back.

As you talk, casually bring your right hand back to the edge of the table and then down to your lap. Without glancing down, pick the glass up and move it to the left so that it's under the bottom of your jacket. "You're probably wondering what happened to the glass. So was I: actually, it hasn't gone far at all." Raise the right hand, still holding the glass, up inside the left side of your jacket. The right forearm is across the body but the hand and glass are hidden from view inside the jacket **(6)**.

Move your hand level with your inside jacket pocket and pretend to be rummaging around inside for a moment, then bring the glass out into view as if you've just removed it from your inside pocket **(7)**. Done smoothly and with a little acting skill, it really does look as if the glass reappeared inside there. ✋

PAPER CHASE

The sleight-of-hand master strikes again with this cute impromptu routine. Three balled-up pieces of paper behave in an amazing manner – every time you put one of them away in your pocket it magically jumps back to your other hand. You offer to do the trick more slowly. This time, not only does it make a reappearance but it's grown to a monster size!

The secret of this trick is that while the spectators are only aware of three small paper balls, in fact you have a fourth. The extra ball, combined with some simple sleight-of-hand, creates the illusion that the ball always returns to the hand.

Make the paper balls ahead of time by tearing up a napkin into quarters and rolling each piece up as tightly as possible. For the finale, make up a larger ball from a whole napkin, or even two or three napkins (1). You don't have to use paper balls for this trick; you can make them out of silver foil, or use olives, cherries, dice or anything else to hand. And for the finale try using a completely different object – an egg, a lemon, a large die; anything which will create a surprise.

Begin the routine with the three balls on the table. The fourth one is classic-palmed in your right hand. The large ball is in your right jacket pocket. "Here's a strange thing," you say, "I don't know why it happens: it just does. Maybe you can explain it. It uses these paper balls. Watch: I put one, two in my hand and one in the pocket." As you say this, the right hand picks up one of the paper balls and places it in your left hand. It then picks up a second paper ball but, as it places this in your left hand, it allows the classic-

palmed ball to fall with it **(2)**. The left hand closes over the three balls so that the spectator can't see or count them. "And I place one in the pocket." Your right hand picks up the remaining ball from the table, holds it up so that everyone can see it and then places it in the right jacket pocket. However, as soon as the hand is out of sight, the ball is classic-palmed. "And yet, when I open my hand, there are still three balls." Open the left hand and let the three balls roll out on to the table **(3)**. "I just don't get it! Let me have another go."

Repeat the entire sequence. Place two balls into your left hand and secretly add the palmed ball to them. Then pick up the ☞

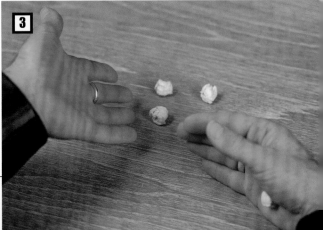

third ball and pretend to place it in your right jacket pocket, but actually palm it. Open your hand to show that once again the three balls have returned. "Drives me mad… I think it might have something to do with this ball here." Pick up any one of the balls and place it aside. "Keep your eye on that one." Then pick up the other two balls, one at a time, and place them in your left hand, the same as before. Again, you secretly add the palmed ball to them.

"This is the dodgy one." Pick up the remaining ball from the table and show it briefly before placing it in the right jacket pocket.

This time, leave the ball in the pocket; the right hand comes out empty, so casually let the spectators see that. Then open your left hand to reveal that, once again, it holds three balls. Drop the balls on to the table. "Am I doing it too fast? Let's try it this way. I'll take one ball and place it in my pocket." The right hand picks up a ball and really does place it in the right jacket pocket. "Then I put one in my hand." You pick up another ball in your right hand and appear to place it in your left. In fact, you secretly retain it in your right.

To do this, hold the ball between the thumb and fingers (4). As your right hand approaches the left one, it appears to drop the ball into the left hand. In reality, though, the ball drops on to the right fingers where it can be finger-palmed (5).

There's a knack to making this look natural. Just do the move at the same rhythm you've been using throughout. Don't hesitate: just pick the ball up, apparently drop it into the left hand, then close the left fingers around it as the right hand moves away with the ball hidden in the curl of its fingers. The right hand picks up the last ball between thumb and forefinger (6).

The curled right fingers hide the palmed ball. Say, "And the last one goes in the pocket." Hold the last ball up so that everyone can see it and then put it away in your right jacket pocket. "So that's two in the pocket: how many in the hand?" As the spectators ponder

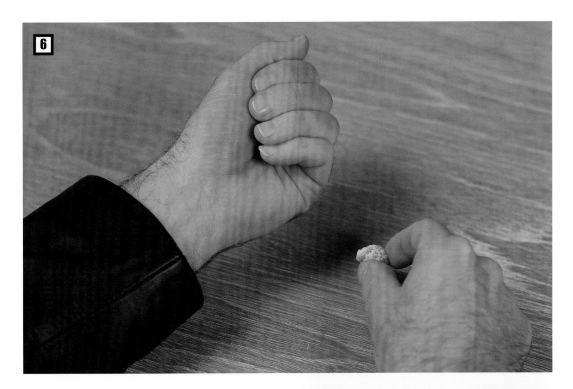

this unexpected question you drop the two balls held in the right hand and pick up the large ball that's in the pocket.

Classic-palm it or just hold it in a finger-palm position as you bring your hand out of the pocket; use whichever hold you feel most comfortable with. It's difficult to know what answer the spectators might give to your question; they could say anything from "One ball" to "Three balls" to "None". No matter what they say, ask a spectator to place their hands together and hold them palm-upwards. As soon as they've done that, providing you with a makeshift tabletop, you bring the left and right hand up together.

They're held directly above the spectator's hands. Your right hand is slightly below the left. Open both hands at once, allowing the large ball to drop on to theirs **(7)**. Its appearance should be a complete surprise. "Now, that's the bit that gets me!"

NOTES
The joy of this routine is that you can do it with almost any small objects and vary the storyline. It looks good, too, if you create a kind of suspended table out of a cloth napkin or scarf or even a borrowed jacket: have a spectator either side of you, each one taking two corners, one in each hand, and stretching it out in front of you. Use this as your work surface; it'll provide a soft landing for any object you produce, especially something fragile such as an egg.

CAP DANCING CLUB

The spectators won't believe their eyes when you perform this trick. You arrange four bottle caps on the table so that each is at the corner of an imaginary square. Wave your hands over two of them and one travels across invisibly to join the other – then another and another until all four bottle caps are together in one corner. Weird.

This trick goes back a long way in magical history. It's been performed with dice, sugar cubes, corks and coins, but I prefer to use bottle caps because it makes it a natural bar or party trick. They should all be identical and you need to be able to classic-palm them, which is really easy if you have them upside-down with the serrated edge uppermost – another good reason to use bottle caps.

Although the trick appears to use four bottle caps, it actually uses five. One of them is hidden, classic-palmed in your right hand before the trick begins. Take the other four caps and arrange them open-side-up in a square formation **(1)**.

"This is a test of whether or not you're sober: if you understand it, you're not. Four bottle caps, two hands, no safety net." Cover one of the caps with your right hand and one with your left. Then lift the hands and move them around to cover two different caps. Wiggle your fingers each time you cover a cap. All this does is get the spectators

3

used to the movements you'll be making later and helps convince them nothing is used in this trick apart from your two hands and the four caps. Now put the left hand over the cap at the lower left corner nearest you, and the right hand over the cap at the upper right corner.

Wiggle your fingers and press your left hand down on to the cap so that it becomes gripped in classic-palm position. At the same time, place your right hand down and quietly drop its cap alongside the one already there. Instantly lift both your hands, retaining the cap in your left hand palm. Move your hands to either side so that the spectators can see what's happened. It appears that the cap on the left has magically jumped to join the one on the right **(2)**.

Quickly place your left hand on to the cap at the upper left and drop the palmed cap next to the one already there. At the same time, place your right hand over the cap at the lower right corner.

Wiggle your fingers and lift your hands and move them aside as before, but this time palming the cap covered by the right hand. It looks like another cap has magically teleported across the table and this time appeared at the upper left corner **(3)**.

The caps are on the move. "They love to get together and party." Let the spectators take this in for a moment and then position the left hand over the two caps at the upper left corner. Move the right hand over the caps at the upper right and drop its palmed cap there. Wiggle your fingers again while palming a cap in the left hand, and then move the hands aside. Another cap has travelled across: there are now three of them at the upper right corner **(4)**.

"I've no idea what they put in the drinks here, but it seems to be working. One more cap to go: let's do this one the hard way." Pick the cap up in the right hand, toss it into the air and catch it. Place your left hand over the three caps on the table, dropping its palmed cap next to them. "Right through the table this time: watch."

Show the cap in the right hand and then take it under the table. Secretly drop it into your lap as you extend your hand under the table to a position directly below the left one. "Here goes!" Bang the right hand against the underside of the table as if knocking the cap through. Bring your hand out empty and then raise the left hand to show that all four bottle caps are now together **(5)**. "Any questions?" ☞

NOTES

Performed at speed, this is a bewildering trick. It's like watching trick photography taking place live before your very eyes. The key is to be able to do the palming smoothly. Dropping the palmed caps is easy: just make sure that your hand is flat on the tabletop so the cap doesn't make a tell-tale noise as you drop it.

You can vary the finish; you could pick up the cap in the right hand, saying, "Of course, it's all done with the sleeves." Reach inside your jacket and pretend to drop the cap into the top of the left sleeve. Really, you drop it into your inside jacket pocket. The left hand covers the three caps on the table.

With the right hand pointing to your shoulder, say, "The cap starts here and slides down to the elbow – wheee! Oops, having a little trouble there…" Tug at the elbow as if freeing a jammed bottle cap and then continue to describe its imaginary journey down the forearm and along under the wrist. Wiggle the left fingers and raise the hand to show that it's now joined the other three.

There's another handling you can use to make the ending even more interesting. It's not 100 per cent sure-fire, but when it works it looks great. When you place the left hand over the caps for the last move, don't cover them all completely. As your left hand drops the final cap, your thumb should be just forward of the cap nearest to you. When you pretend to push the fourth cap through the table, lift your left hand slightly and then slam it down on to the caps. Your left thumb catches the far edge of that innermost cap and sends it spinning into the air. From the front, no one notices that the jumping cap is one of the ones which was already there. It really looks as if a bottle cap has just flown right up through the table!

OVER THEIR HEAD

You crumple a paper napkin up into a ball and place it into your left hand. A spectator watches you like a hawk – and yet the paper ball completely disappears. You tell him to watch more closely, screw up another napkin and place it into your hand again. He doesn't take his eyes off it, but that ball disappears too. In fact, you can spend all night making those paper balls vanish and he won't have a clue where they go.

It must be magic.

This is one of the funniest tricks in magic because, while your hawk-eyed victim might not have any idea where those paper balls are going, the rest of the audience do! That's because they can see that you're simply throwing them backwards over his head and therefore out of range of his vision.

Let me take you through the handling. You can do this trick anywhere but it's easier if your volunteer is sitting down, whether on a bench in the park or a chair in a restaurant. If you decide to do the trick standing up, try to pick someone who's shorter than you.

The key thing is that your hands are at the volunteer's eye level as you hold up the paper ball. You'll see why in a moment. You can make anything that won't make a giveaway noise as it hits the deck behind them disappear! Paper napkins, toilet roll or torn-up newspaper are ideal but I've done it with fruit, bread rolls and even snowballs! Let's imagine that your volunteer is seated. You're standing to his left. He has a stack of napkins on his lap. You take one of the napkins and crumple it up into a ball **(1)**.

The ball is held in the right hand level with his chest as you say, "This is very simple. Just keep your eye on the left hand: that's where the action is." Hold your left hand palm-up in front of him. "I'm going to count to three: keep your eyes on the hand and on the ball." Raise the right hand and the ball as you count "One" and then quickly bring the ball back down to the left hand in a clapping motion. Raise the ball again as you count "Two." Again, bring the ball back down to the left hand. Finally, as you raise the ball a third time, release it on the upward swing so that it sails right over ☞

the spectator's head and out of his view **(2)**.

Without pausing, count "Three" and bring the empty right hand down to the left hand. Pretend to take the ball with the left hand but really just close the left fingers around empty air. Point to the left hand with your right as you say, "Watch the hand, watch the ball: look." Then slowly open both hands and brush them together. To the spectator, it looks as if the ball's dissolved into thin air **(3)**.

Of course, everyone else watching sees the ball fly back over the spectator's head. The trick is no mystery to them, but if you look at them and give them a sly wink, they'll usually keep quiet about the secret. Everyone loves to be in on a gag and see a mate suckered. Put a finger to your lips to shush anyone who might feel compelled to laugh a little too loudly. The seated spectator shouldn't see any signals that you give to the rest of the audience – this is easily covered by the fact that they're seated below and slightly forward of you.

"Just in case you didn't get that," you say to your bemused spectator, "let me show you again." Take another napkin, squash it into a ball and do the trick once more. It's even funnier for the rest of the audience when the second ball disappears and the spectator still doesn't have a clue as to where it's gone.

You can carry on as long as you like. When the ground behind him is littered with paper, make one final ball disappear. Wrap several napkins together to make an enormous one. It's so big that your hands won't cover it, so he might spot it going over his head. If so, it really doesn't matter; it's a final big laugh as he finally cottons on to what's been happening and turns round to see the mountain of paper behind him. But sometimes you'll manage to fool them even with that huge ball. If so, just thank him for his help and as he goes back to join his friends, stop him in his tracks, saying, "Hey, aren't you going to clear up after yourself?" and point him in the direction of all the paper balls. That's the last laugh of the routine – the priceless look on the poor guy's face.

NOTES

If there are spectators stood right round me, I like to involve them in the final part of the trick. I nod my head towards one of them, signalling him to move directly behind the seated spectator. Then I say to the volunteer, "It's one thing making paper balls disappear, but I think we need a real challenge. Let's try it with one of your shoes." I then persuade him to take one off.

The scenario becomes clear to the second spectator, who's now standing to the rear of the chair. He knows I'm going to throw the shoe into the air and I want him to catch it so that it doesn't make a noise as it hits the floor. An alternative strategy is to set up one of your mates as an accomplice before you even start the trick.

I make exactly the same moves I did with the paper balls and on the count of three the shoe goes soaring into the air. With any luck, your helper behind will catch it and the seated spectator will wonder where the hell it's gone. If he catches you out, it doesn't matter; the whole situation gets a huge laugh anyway. If he doesn't spot it, I send him hopping back to his friends and let them decide when he should get his shoe back. There's always someone who'll hide it behind their back or inside their jacket: it's amazing how quick-thinking people can be when cruelty to friends is involved!

On one of my television shows I performed an even harsher version of this trick. I did it while standing next to a bus shelter. The shoe I made disappear flew high into the air and landed on top of the shelter. It landed with such a loud thud that the spectator jumped and turned around to see what the noise was. There was a lovely moment of realization on their face that not only was it their shoe which had made the noise, but that it was now stuck up there out of reach. Meanwhile, I made a run for it!

SPOON-BENDING

Everyone's heard of so-called psychics who claim they can bend spoons using the power of their minds. Well, now you can do it too. You take an ordinary spoon, stroke it lightly and the metal mysteriously bends; it's an amazingly convincing illusion to watch. But you can go even further than that. You take another spoon and this time it doesn't just bend: it breaks completely in two.

Some people claim to be able to do this for real: I think the technical term for them is "charlatans". A much easier and more practical way to bend and break spoons is to use sleight-of-hand and psychology. There are two secrets to this illusion because the bending and the breaking of the spoon use completely different methods, so let's look at them one at a time.

The Bend

The only requirement is that the spoon you intend to bend using your mysterious "psychic" powers can actually be bent using just your hands. Most spoons are not very strong and can easily be bent using a little brute force. I suggest you start with teaspoons and work your way up the cutlery chain. It's also much better if a trick like this arises out of some natural conversation. If people know you do tricks, and especially if you've already done some mind-reading, they'll almost always want to discuss other strange phenomena.

You won't find it difficult to steer the conversation towards spoon-bending. "Have you seen that freak on TV who bends spoons? Have you ever tried it yourself? No? Let's have a go now, then. Everyone grab a spoon." Involving the whole audience makes this a perfect party trick. When everyone, including you, has a spoon in their hands, the routine begins. "Just hold the spoon in your left hand like this and, with your right fingers, start to stroke it at the neck."

You hold your spoon at the bowl, between the finger and thumb of the left hand **(1)**. The right hand then comes over the top and strokes it at the neck of the spoon **(2)**. Keep stroking it as if genuinely trying to make it bend and encourage the spectators to do the same. Do this for a few moments until you can see that they're all joining in and genuinely occupied with the futile task in hand.

No matter how hard they try, unless they're cheating, no one's spoon will bend, including yours. What you need is a spot of misdirection so that you can secretly put a bend in your spoon.

You get it by looking at one of the spectators near you and saying, "No, not like that: do it like this." You stop stroking your spoon and reach over with your right hand as if to help him.

Keep the bowl of the spoon in the left hand. It's more than likely that most people will be holding theirs the opposite way round to you. Give him some bogus advice about the right position and then

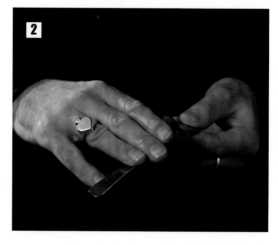

move his hands so that they're closer to what you were demonstrating earlier. Other people nearby will look at his hands to see how they should be holding their spoons. This is your moment of misdirection – they're not watching you; they're watching someone else or checking that they're following your instructions correctly. Time to make your move. "That's better," you say. Your hands take hold of the spoon once again and, when no one is looking, give it a sharp but subtle bend **(3)**.

You need to do this quickly and without giving away the fact that you're using any pressure on the spoon. Use the minimum movement possible and bend it at the neck where it's weakest. Don't suddenly yank at the ends of the spoon as if trying to bend the unbendable. Spoons, particularly teaspoons, require an amazingly small amount of strength to bend. You can even hold it in one hand and lever it against the outside of your thigh if it's a thin, weak one.

Immediately the spoon's bent, return it to the starting position in the left hand with the fingers and thumb on the inverted bowl. The right hand hides the bend from view. The spoon is held at waist height and the handle is pointing towards the spectators. Continue talking as if nothing has changed. "That's good, keep stroking it and

think "Bend!" You'll feel it start to get warm." Do this for a few more seconds and then suddenly say, "It's working! Look, I think it's starting to bend." Everyone will stop what they're doing and look at your spoon. The right hand is still stroking it. When you've got their attention, gradually draw your right fingers off the neck of the spoon, gradually exposing the bend until you're just stroking the neck of the spoon with your middle finger **(4, 5, 6)**. Here's the moment where you convince everyone that the spoon's actually bending before their very eyes. Slowly pull back with the left thumb on the bowl of the spoon. The handle of the spoon will start to tip upwards **(7)**.

"Look – look at the handle!" Everyone will focus on the handle and, as they do, you tip the bowl upwards a little more. The small movement at the bowl of the spoon turns into a larger movement at the handle. The handle slowly rises up an inch or two and it genuinely looks as if the spoon is bending. It's an amazing optical illusion.

If you slowly turn to your left as you do it, the illusion of the movement of the spoon is really strong. You're almost done. "It's bent. It's definitely bent, isn't it?" Stop stroking the spoon and take it in the right hand by the handle. With your left hand, take a ☞

spoon from someone else and hold them both up for everyone to see. The difference is obvious. The only conclusion anyone can come to is that you've just bent a spoon using the power of the mind.

The Break

The breaking spoon is a great follow-up to the bending spoon but it requires a bit of preparation. If you know you're going to do this trick, you need to steal a spoon and prepare it in advance. Take it to the bathroom or somewhere private. Hold it between your hands and bend it up and down rapidly **(8)**.

The spoon will get very hot as you do this, so be careful you don't burn yourself – seriously! The bending fatigues the metal in the spoon, making it weak. You need to bend it backwards and forwards enough times to weaken it but not quite break it. If you've got several spoons, it's worth counting the number of bends you make before one snaps, and then repeating it with another spoon but stopping one bend short. It takes some practice to get that judgement right, but if you do, you'll have a spoon that looks completely normal apart from a small hairline fracture at the neck.

Put it somewhere you can find it easily during the routine: under a napkin, on the table or even in your pocket. Now imagine that you've just performed the bending spoon trick. Everyone's understandably excited. Some people are examining the bent spoon, others are still trying to make their own spoons bend.

You pick up another one – this time it's the one you've prepared earlier – and again you start to show everyone how easy it is to make it bend. Once again you hold the spoon by the bowl and rub it with your right fingers. Everyone's watching you. Rub it for a little while and then say, "Wow, this one's going really fast – quick, hold out your hands." Someone does so and you change the position of the spoon so that you're holding it by the handle in your left hand. Cover the break with your right forefinger and thumb and keep rubbing it there **(9)**.

What you actually do is gradually apply some force with the right thumb and finger, bending the bowl down until it breaks. Sometimes the bowl will just snap off, but sometimes it will dangle for a while as if the neck is melting – this looks great and gets gasps of amazement **(10)**.

Either way, when it does, you let it fall into the spectator's open hands **(11)**. Pretend to be really excited. Your enthusiasm is contagious and it's all part of the atmosphere. You want the audience to feel that something really weird just happened.

NOTES

The most difficult part of the spoon-bending routine is sitting around afterwards with your audience and having to answer all their questions about supposed psychic phenomena!

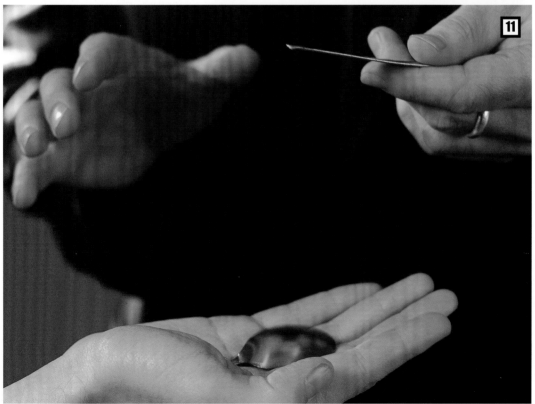

OUT OF THIS WORLD

This is possibly the greatest card trick in the world. By the time you've finished this book you'll be able to do all kinds of miracles, but in this trick it's the spectator who seems to do the magic. Without having any idea as to how she did it, a member of your audience manages to guess the colour of every single face-down card in the pack correctly. This is a reputation-making routine.

The Secret

The trick uses a pre-arranged deck. The first eight cards of the face-down deck are a mixture of black and red cards, in any order. They're followed by the rest of the red cards. And below them are the remainder of the black cards **(1)**. I'll divide the trick into steps to make the working clear.

Proving that the Cards are Mixed

Apart from the top eight cards, the deck is divided into reds and blacks, but you'll need to convince the spectators that the deck is mixed. You say, "Let's try an experiment in intuition. Since females are supposedly more intuitive than males, would you help?" Choose a girl from the audience. "But then you probably knew I'd choose you, didn't you? We're going to play a guessing game. All I want you to do is guess whether a card you're holding face-down is a red one or a black one."

Spread through the deck and take out one red card and one black card from somewhere around the middle. Make sure that no

This trick is called Out of This World and was first devised in the 1940s by American magician Paul Curry. Its elegant and clever method created a sensation among magicians, while its effect made it a favourite with audiences. During the Second World War, magician Harry Green performed it for the British Prime Minister Winston Churchill. Harry loved card tricks and must have performed this one incredibly well, because Churchill asked him to do it again. As a magician, you wouldn't normally do the same trick twice for an audience, but then you wouldn't normally be asked to do it again by a Prime Minister. Even after a second performance, Churchill was completely baffled, so he asked Harry to do it again. And again.

In fact Harry Green performed the trick no fewer than six times in all, and at the end Churchill was as baffled as the first time. He was also late for his next meeting and didn't arrive at Parliament until two in the morning!

one sees the arrangement in the deck as you do this. These two cards will be your marker cards. Place both cards face-up on the table, the red to your right and the black to your left. The spectator is sitting opposite you. "Let me show you what I mean. Here are two marker cards, one red, one black," you say, pointing at the cards you've just placed down. Then point to the top card of the deck. "If you feel this card is a black one, put it face-down here." You deal the card face-down on to the face-up black card. "And if you think this card is a red card, deal it here." You deal the next card from the deck on to the face-up red card. "And then continue dealing through the deck, each time making a guess as to whether the top card is red or black and dealing it on to the appropriate pile."

You continue guessing your way through the next six cards of the deck to demonstrate. All the cards dealt are coming from the mixed bunch of cards. "Understand? Good, let's start."

You now take the eight cards you've just dealt and turn them face-up. The spectators will see they're a mixture of reds and blacks. Your guessing probably won't have been spot-on, so some will have been dealt on to the wrong marker cards. That's fine. "I'm not very good at this!" you explain as you move the wrong-colour cards across to their correct marker cards. "These should have been over here."

Pick up all the red cards except the marker and casually place them somewhere in the top half of the deck. They go in among all the other red cards which are stacked there. Now pick up all the black cards, with the exception of the marker again, and place them in the lower half of the deck which, unknown to the audience, is entirely made up of black cards. This introductory demonstration not only explains what's going to happen but also subtly convinces the spectators that the cards are mixed.

The Spectator Guesses

Hand the deck to the spectator, saying, "Now it's your turn. No need to rush: take your time. If you think a card's red, deal it on the red card there. If you think it's black, put it on the black one. No cheating!" The spectator starts to deal the cards; some on to the red marker and

some on to the black one **(2)**. Keep a mental count of how many cards she's dealing. One of the reasons you tell her not to deal quickly is so that you can keep track of the number of cards. Anticipate the 24th card coming up and, as she deals it, ask her to stop.

There are 26 red cards in a deck; if you add the marker card to the 24 she's dealt, that means there's only one more red card left. You're about to make use of that. "You're doing very well: maybe a bit too well. Let me try to confuse you a little." Take the deck back from her and give it a quick shuffle. "That should do it."

Spread the deck out towards you so that only you can see the faces and remove the solitary red card and also any random black card. "Let's use two different cards as markers." Place the red one on top of the left-hand pile and the black one on to the right-hand pile **(3)**. "You can see that I've switched the marker cards round. Now, if you think a card's red, deal it over here this time; if you think it's black, put it here. Off you go." The spectator continues dealing out the rest of the deck on to the two new markers until there are none left **(4)**.

The Finale

If you turned over the right-hand pile on the table now and spread them out the spectator would be amazed to see that she has in fact guessed all the cards correctly – placing all the red cards on to the red marker card and all the black cards on to the black one.

This is purely a result of the dealing process. Unfortunately, things wouldn't look so good if you did the same with left pile. All the dealt cards are on the wrong markers. We'll deal with that potential problem in a moment. Square up that packet of cards and move them to one side without comment, then turn your attention to the right-hand packet.

Spread the cards face-down in a line across the table **(5)**. Point out the black marker card in the middle. "If you thought that a card was black you dealt it here, right? Turn the cards above it face-up, one at a time, and put them over here." The spectator starts turning the cards face-up and placing them into a pile at the side of the table where you indicated **(6)**. All the cards will be black. ☞

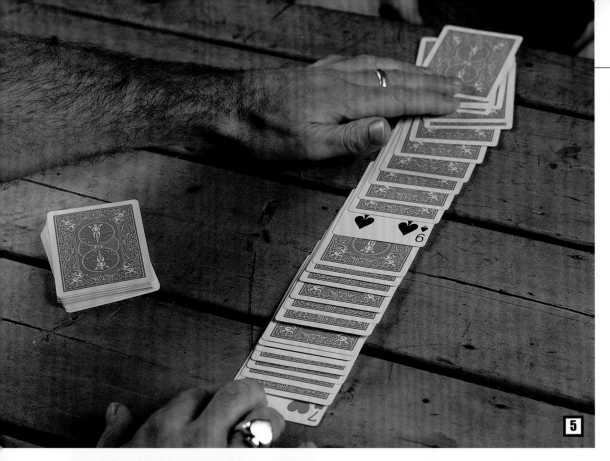

5

6

It looks as if all the spectator's guesses are correct and she'll be suitably baffled. Slide the black marker card across to the newly-created face-up pile of black cards. Point out the remaining red marker card and the line of face-down cards above it. "Turn them over, one at a time; let's see how many red cards you managed to guess right." She deals the cards into a separate pile next to the face-up black cards **(7)**.

Every guess she made is correct and every single card is red. She and everyone else will be amazed: so amazed that they won't really be paying attention to what you do next. Pick up the "wrong" pile of

cards you placed aside earlier. Spread it face-down between your hands and remove the two marker cards. Casually toss the red card on to the face-up red pile already on the table and the black card on to the face-up black pile. Now turn the rest of the packet face-up and with a sweep of the hand spread the packet in a wide arc, saying, "And if those were right, chances are you got these right too."

Everyone can see the spread divided into reds and blacks **(8)**. No one will spot that they're actually in the wrong order, the reds having been dealt below the blacks. Your experiment in intuition has been an out-of-this-world success.

NOTES

It'd be embarrassing if you picked up the wrong pile at the finish. To prevent that, there's an easy way of remembering which pile is right. It's all to do with the letter "R" – the Right pile is on the Right. And you know it's right because it starts with a red card and red starts with "R". You might not need it, but it's helped me remember!

There's also a great bit of business you can use during this trick. All the cards dealt after the second set of markers are black. Any time the spectator deals a card on to the second red marker, you can stop her and say, "You thought that one was a red card?" She'll say "Yes." You say, "Sorry: you've been doing really well so far but I'm not entirely sure you're right with that one." Turn the card over and show that it's actually a black one. Place it aside until the trick's finished. It's a great way of convincing the spectator even more that the cards are mixed.

Magicians have devised many different ways of cleaning up the "wrong" pile at the end of this trick. The one described here works for me, but don't be afraid to come up with your own.

If I were going to recommend any addition to this routine, then I'd think about an overhand false shuffle before the trick begins. Just make sure you undercut less than half the deck so that you're only taking black cards. Draw the top card of the right packet off on to the cards in the left hand, injogging it. Shuffle the rest of the right-hand cards on top of the injog. Finish by cutting the deck at the injog and complete the cut.

Don't draw attention to the shuffle: just do it as you're chatting about the forthcoming experiment in intuition. Later, if anyone tries to work out how the trick's done, they'll remember that you shuffled the cards before you started. And one thing's for sure: you can't do this trick with a shuffled deck. Enjoy.

GLOSSARY

Magic has its own jargon; technical words for the secret moves, principles and equipment that are commonly used in the craft. This glossary will hopefully serve as a useful reminder of the meaning of the terms used in this book.

BOTTOM OF THE DECK
When the cards are held face-down in the left hand, the bottom of the deck will be the lowermost card. Sometimes magicians call this the face card of the deck.

BREAK
A break is a secret gap held between cards in the deck, usually by a finger. It's used when controlling the whereabouts of a certain card, usually one chosen by the spectator.

CLASSIC PALM
Used to conceal a small object, most commonly a coin, in the hand by secretly holding it between the muscles at the base of the thumb and the lower edge of the hand.

CONTROL
Magicians talk of controlling a spectator's selected card. It means that although they to appear to lose it in the deck, they know exactly where it is and can often bring it to the top with a single cut. Key Cards and Breaks are used to affect Controls.

CRIMP
A bend made in the corner of a card so that it can be easily located visually or by touch and then Controlled. The bent corner makes it easy to cut at the crimped card. Magicians talk about putting a crimp in a card and also refer to the bent card itself as a crimp.

DEAL
To take the cards, one at a time from the top of the deck and place them on the table. The cards can be dealt in a pile on the table. In a gambling routine the cards would be dealt around the table, cards going to each player's hand in clockwise rotation.

DEALING GRIP
This is the grip that most people use when holding a deck of cards ready to deal for a card game. The deck is face-down in the left hand. The fingers are on the right long side of the deck. The thumb lies across the top of the deck. Occasionally the forefinger is on the front edge of the deck. In this book I sometimes refer to the deck being held in the left-hand dealing grip. Card cheats refer to this as the Mechanic's Grip, a mechanic being a slang term for a card cheat.

DECK
Another name for a pack of cards. Magicians usually use the term deck when talking card tricks. It's an American term that's become widespread among magicians worldwide who specialise in card magic.

DOUBLE LIFT
This is a Sleight in which two cards are lifted as though they are one and turned over on top of the deck. It can be used to change one card into another as in the Stabbed in the Deck trick, and it's used several times in the Ambitious Card Routine, both of which are found in the Shark Attack chapter.

FACE-DOWN
If a card is dealt face-down onto the table it means that the back pattern is uppermost; the opposite of Face-Up.

FACE-UP
This refers to a card having the face side uppermost so that its value can be seen; the opposite to Face-Down.

FALSE SHUFFLE
A shuffle that controls the position of some or all of the cards in the deck. You might have a Key Card on the bottom of the deck. A false shuffle apparently mixes the cards up, but in fact afterwards the Key Card is still at the bottom of the deck.

FINGER PALM
This refers to when a coin or other small object is hidden in the curl of the fingers; it is finger-palmed.

FLOURISH
A deliberately visual and fancy move, usually with a deck of cards.

FORCE
When a magician forces an item it means that although the spectator appears to have a free choice of several or numerous items (often a card from the deck), in fact they have none. Although they won't know it, they'll end taking the object or card that the magician wanted them to take.

FRENCH DROP
This is a Sleight used to make a coin vanish. The coin is held at the fingertips of one hand and then apparently taken away with the other. In fact it's retained in the original hand where it's then usually Palmed, out of sight of the spectators.

GIMMICK

A hidden Prop that the spectators don't know about, such as the nail writer described in On the Nail in the Top Secret Gadgets chapter. Magicians also talk about items being gimmicked; the fake coin used in Smoke and Mirrors, also in the Top Secret Gimmicks chapter, could be described as a gimmicked coin.

INJOG

When a card protrudes out of the pack towards the performer it's said to be injogged; this can be done during an Overhand Shuffle.

KEY CARD

A key card is a known card that indicates the position of a spectator's selected card. For instance you might known that the ace of spades is the bottom card of the deck. During the trick you contrive to get the ace of spades right next to the spectator's chosen card. You now know that whatever card is next to the ace of spades is the selection. See Card Crime in the Hands on Deck chapter.

MATE

A mate of a card is one of the same value and colour but different suit - the mate of the Jack of clubs is the Jack of spades and the mate of the eight of hearts would be the eight of diamonds.

MISDIRECTION

Redirecting the audience's attention to something other than the method of the trick. You might gaze at the left hand following a French Drop, to encourage the audience to believe that a coin is there. Looking in the direction of the left hand discourages the audience from looking at the right hand where the coin is actually palmed.

OUTJOG

When a card protrudes out of the pack away from the performer, it's known as an outjog. A card can be outjogged during an Overhand Shuffle although this is rarely used because an outjog can be seen by

the spectators; an Injog is therefore far more commonly used.

OVERHAND SHUFFLE

This is the most common way of shuffling cards. The right hand picks up the deck, holding it at the narrow ends, and the left thumb pulls cards off, generally in small batches, into its hand. The shuffle continues until all the cards are in the left hand and now in a different order.

PACKET

A packet of cards is a small quantity of playing cards. You can cut a packet of cards from the deck or you can deal cards into a packet on the table.

PALM

This not only refers to part of the hand, but is used in magic to describe the Sleight in which an object is concealed in the hand. You palm a coin; the action is referred to as palming. There are several different types of palming – see Classic Palm and Finger Palm.

PREDICTION

If you foretell the future you're making a prediction. Mind-readers might, for instance, write down the name of a card that hasn't yet been chosen and refer to it as a prediction.

PROPS

Any objects you use to perform tricks with.

REVELATION

Magicians talk about the revelation at the end of a trick. This might be the discovery or naming of a selected card. Or revealing of a prediction. It denotes the finale

ROUTINE

If a trick involves more than one phase magicians might call it a routine. For instance if you combine an appearing coin trick with a vanishing coin trick, you might claim to have created a routine.

SELECTION

The card or other object that the spectator chooses.

SLEIGHT

A secret move which brings about the magic or facilitates the trick.

SLEIGHT OF HAND

Manual dexterity in the performance of magic. People often refer to the quickness of the hands but speed is rarely of value in magic. More useful is the ability to act naturally while Palming or executing some other complex move.

SHUFFLE

Means to mix the cards. There are lots of different types of shuffle, the most common of which is the Overhand Shuffle.

SLEEVING

When a magician secretly sends a coin or other small object up his sleeve it's known as sleeving. Generally it's used to affect a vanish - you sleeve the coin.

TOP OF THE DECK

When the cards are held face-down in the left hand, the top of the deck is the uppermost card.

TOP STOCK

A stock of cards is a group or block of cards. The top stock therefore is a group of cards on top of the deck. The term is often used when describing how cards are controlled during a false shuffle. The magician might secretly arrange four aces on top of the deck – the aces are the top stock. A false shuffle is then used to apparently mix the cards but in fact the top stock is retained; the aces are still on top of the deck.

UPJOG

If you spread through the deck and raise each ace, for example, as you come to it so that all the aces are sticking up and out of the spread, magicians say that the aces are upjogged. If you were looking for four aces in the deck you'd spread through the cards, upjog the aces and then pull them out all at once before placing them on the table.

RETAILERS ETC...

Here's a short guide to further information about magic and magicians, their websites, publications and suppliers.

MAGIC ON THE INTERNET

Magic has a large profile on the Internet; search engines such as Google will lead you to hundreds of sites, but here are a couple of good places to begin your exploration:

Magic Week
A British website updated weekly with the latest news, links to 'dealers' and discussion groups.
www.magicweek.co.uk

All Magic Guide
A U.S. based web site that provides a good launching pad to the world of magic and magicians and has the bonus of featuring some magic tutorials.
www.allmagic.com

MAGIC CONVENTIONS AND SOCIETIES

Many towns and cities have their own magic society where magicians meet to swap tricks, gossip and watch lectures by visiting magicians. They also sometimes have conventions; usually once a year, where they stage larger-scale shows and have numerous dealers peddling their wares. While the conventions can be fun, I'd actually advise against joining a society. That might sound a little odd, but in my experience these organizations tend to encourage the wrong kind of development; the emphasis is too much on technique rather than presentation. One gets the impression that many members of magic societies end up just trying to impress and outdo each other in terms of advanced "moves" rather than concentrating on entertaining non-magicians.

MAGIC DEALERS

Every large town or city used to have it's own magic store where books and equipment could be bought but the Internet has revolutionized the distribution of information about magic, as with everything else. Here are the addresses of some of the most prominent dealers in props, books and DVDs.

Dealers based in the U.K:

Magic Tricks
www.magictricks.co.uk

Alakazam Magic
www.alakazam.co.uk

House of Secrets
www.houseofsecrets.co.uk

Dealers based in the U.S:

Hank Lee's Magic Factory
www.hanklee.org

Hocus Pocus Magic
www.hocus-pocus.com

MAGIC MAGAZINES

Magicians have their own trade journals featuring news, articles, tricks and advertising from magic 'dealers'. Here are a few of the most popular:

Magic Seen
Bi-monthly magazine published in the U.K.
www.magicseen.co.uk

Magic
A monthly magazine published in the U.S.
www.magicmagazine.com

Genii
A monthly magazine published in the U.S.
www.geniimagazine.com